Learning

Best Accelerated Learning Tips to Improve
Memory and Speed Reading, Enhance Intellect

(Memory Improvement for Beginners, Adult and
Linguists)

Peter Meier

Published by Rob Miles

© **Peter Meier**

All Rights Reserved

Learning: Best Accelerated Learning Tips to Improve Memory and Speed Reading, Enhance Intellect (Memory Improvement for Beginners, Adult and Linguists)

ISBN 978-1-7771171-1-5

Legal & Disclaimer

The information contained in this book is not designed to replace or take the place of any form of medicine or professional medical advice. The information in this book has been provided for educational and entertainment purposes only.

The information contained in this book has been compiled from sources deemed reliable, and it is accurate to the best of the Author's knowledge; however, the Author cannot guarantee its accuracy and validity and cannot be held liable for any errors or omissions. Changes are periodically made to this book. You must consult your doctor or get professional medical advice before using any of the suggested remedies, techniques, or information in this book.

Table of Contents

Introduction

This book contains proven steps and strategies on how to cut the learning curve by implementing the same techniques used by highly successful individuals.

As we all know, our educational system is broken. It was designed to suit the needs of the industrial age and is ineffective at teaching us essential life skills and principles to achieve our fullest potential. It has never been more useless to memorize trivial facts when we have the worlds informational database at our fingertips. The world is changing exponentially as we enter the fourth industrial revolution, yet our primary learning method is still stuck in the 19th century. We must adapt to these dynamic times by pursuing a life-long education that values timeless principles and skills over remembering pointless facts.

Learning is a skill that requires good technique and discipline to master. In this book, I will teach you what the most successful people in the world know about the learning process and the systems they use to cut their learning curve. I will teach you the best techniques on how to learn any skill, improve your memory, double your reading speed, and become more productive instantly.

Thanks again for downloading this book, I hope you enjoy it and apply these techniques into your own life!

Chapter 1: Improving Your Memory

When it comes to learning anything, having an excellent memory is crucial. Without it, you might as well ditch all efforts to learn. After all, learning means nothing if you can't retain what you have just taken in.

It's worth noting however, that what you need is a sufficient memory and not necessarily a perfect one. A sufficient memory can very much be achieved, while a perfect one is only gifted to a special few. So when gunning for an excellent memory, always know that it is achievable and it should be based on you and not on other people. Comparing with others will do you no good. Remember that the only person you are trying to beat every day is you alone. There is no other competition.

Developing a sufficient memory – as well as learning how to learn anything – takes time and practice. Don't expect it to be achieved in a short span of time. It takes work, but the beautiful thing about consistency is that it breeds excellence, including the area of memory.

Mind Exercise

The brain must be treated as a muscle, continually exercise it and strength gains are bound to appear. Though it isn't a physical one, you can undoubtedly develop its power and ability much like you can do with your chest or leg muscles. Just like a muscle, the brain also possesses similar muscle memory that is used to perform certain movements well such as shooting a basketball or kicking a football.

Failure to consistently use or exercise a muscle can lead to a condition known as atrophy, which is the shrinkage in mass and strength. While your brain won't literally shrink due to lack of exercise, your mental performance, strength, and abilities may do so. Hence the importance of exercising your mind often and with intensity.

What goes with the mind also goes hand in hand with your memory. Hence, keeping your mind active can help you improve your memory to reach new heights.

So how does one exercise the mind for developing an excellent memory? There are many ways to do so but in general, here are 4 principles to start off:

1.New Material

Variety is a significant contributor in terms of making your brain more adaptable and staying flexible over the long term. Mental plateaus, decreased cognitive performance, and a weaker memory are some of the main effects of an inability to learn something new every so often. You will need to be exposing yourself to new and unfamiliar information to keep the brain alert and elastic. The more you learn, the easier it becomes for the brain to absorb as it gets used to the regular activity of working itself out.

2. Mental Challenges

The best exercises for your mind are those that compel you to focus. Being challenged isn't enough for your mental exercises or activities – it must require you to focus your mind much more than you normally do. Examples of these are learning a new language or learning to play a new musical instrument. These types of task require the participation of multiple segments in the brain. Deep inside the temporal lobe of the brain lies the limbic system, which dictates your memory. It is through the constant activation of this system that increases memory capacity.

3. Baby Steps

The best mind exercises to help you develop an excellent memory are those that progress one step at a time instead doing so in only one big swoop. Learning something piece by piece over time is certainly more effective than learning the same huge amount of information in just one sitting. By learning one step or topic at a time, you put yourself in the position to achieve many small victories that build up over time and allow you to establish strong foundations for succeeding. The benefits of this approach also gives your brain a sense of achievement every time you are able to advance a small step forward, which leads us into the next principle.

4. Fulfillment:

If the mental or mind exercises you are doing give off a sense of fulfillment or reward to you, chances are that you'll find it easier – desirable even – to continue with them until they bear fruit. If not, your risk of dropping out and failing to enjoy the outcomes associated with the exercises increase significantly. That is why big leaps are not always the most efficient way to learn and strengthen memory. The more effective strategy would be to be patient and steadily work your way up.

In the succeeding chapters, you'll learn many of these exercises that not only help you develop an excellent memory but aid you in learning practically anything with a much higher dexterity.

Let's Get Physical

Exercising your mind can certainly help you achieve significant improvements in terms of cognitive and mental performance, which includes memory. But if you want to really amp up your memory development efforts, consider adding actual physical exercises into the mix. Physical exertion has been proven to help you improve mental sharpness and memory by increasing blood circulation and oxygen delivery to the brain.

Exercising regularly also helps you reduce stress hormones while increasing the good effects of particular brain chemicals such as endorphins. These chemicals secreted by the brain trigger a positive sensation similar to the effects of morphine and also acts as a natural painkiller. Furthermore, exercising regularly assists in keeping the neuroplasticity of your brain's neurons by facilitating new connections between neurons as well as helping in the production of certain growth factors.

When it comes to physical exertion, aerobic exercises are of particular importance. This is because aerobic exercises contribute greatly when it comes to improving blood flow to your brain by making your heart a stronger and more efficient pump. As such, exercises that promote better heart health and strength are considered very useful for encouraging optimal brain performance.

The time of day at which you exercise also plays a significant role in developing an excellent memory. When it comes to timing, the best is exercising in the morning. Beginning your day on the right foot is crucial for setting the tone for the next several hours, especially when it comes to developing an excellent memory. If you're the type of person who seems to struggle hard on most mornings, it would do you well to start the day with an energized boost from a run.

More than just helping you develop excellent memory, morning exercises can also help you feel much better and minimize your risks for a dreaded afternoon or after lunch slump. As mentioned earlier, the real reason why aerobic exercises help you develop excellent memory and optimize mental performance is improved blood circulation. And when it comes to performing such exercises, you don't even need to do these at the gym during your lunch break. You can simply go for a 20-minute brisk walk around the block or in the mall near your office to allow you to experience optimal mental performance for the future.

Sleeping for memory

Make no mistake about it, I adore coffee, especially a strong brew. I find that it helps me go through especially sluggish days and when needed every now and then, a busy night. But despite my deep love and affection for coffee and its ability to keep me awake and alert, I have realized that no amount of the stuff can make me feel as awake and alert throughout the day as an adequate amount of quality sleep. Whenever I get sufficient sleep during the night, I feel awake and alert throughout the day and am able to accomplish what I need to do even without a single sip of coffee. It's just that taking coffee helps give me that extra edge, though it's not the foundation for outstanding mental performance.

Now for most people, 8 hours seem to be the perceived requirement. However, it's not necessarily true. While it is a good starting point for gauging your optimal sleeping hours, it won't be unusual to find that you may need more or less than 8 hours of sleep every night.

So how do you know how much sleep you really need for developing optimal cognitive ability? A good way to do this is by journaling your sleep for the next two weeks. In your journal, write down the time you slept at night and the time you woke up in the morning. Also note the number of hours you slept that evening and how you generally felt all throughout the day, taking particular notice of those days where you felt sluggish, sleepy, and unable to focus mentally. Within two weeks, you will get a pretty accurate idea about your minimum requirement of sleep.

If you're having a difficult time getting quality sleep at night, you may consider the following:

Regular sleeping schedule: Believe it or not, the ability to enjoy quality sleep consistently is dependent to a large extent on sleeping and waking up at roughly the same times every night and every day. Humans and all organisms on the planet work around habits. Be consistent with your sleep and your body and mind will thank you for it. So do your best to sleep at the same time every night and wake up at the same time every morning (even on the weekends!)

Turn your screens off: One of the biggest culprits for the inability to enjoy a good night's sleep is the light emission from TV screens, computer screens, and all other electronic screens. Exposing your eyes to such lights in the evening makes it harder for you to sleep because doing so suppresses your body's ability to release melatonin, which is an important sleep hormone. On top of that, the white light also triggers your body's wake up mechanisms, which can induce much hated insomnia. That is why if you're serious about being able mentally perform at your absolute best, you will have to give up the bad habit of looking at your electronics at least 30 minutes before bedtime.

Ditch The Caffeine: If you love a cup of coffee late in the afternoon and find it hard to sleep at night, it goes without saying that you should stop drinking coffee past 3 or 4 in the afternoon. While some people seem to sleep easily with caffeine, most people don't. And chances are, you may be one of them. So for a deep and restful sleep, stop the late afternoon cups.

Chapter 2:How Human Memory Works

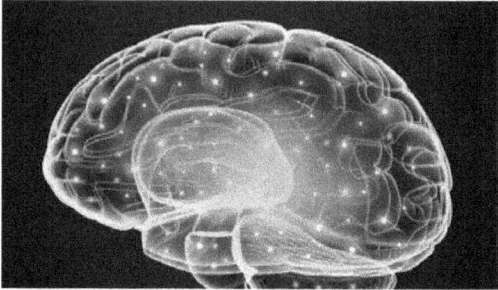

Many folks think of memories as a simple method that allows our minds to recall past events. However, the concept of memory doesn't just involve the past.

Memory is a process where information and data are encoded into our minds in such ways that it is stored and can later be retrieved.

Even though memory is something that we all possess, it does not exist in ways that other parts of our body exist. Memory is not something we can touch because it is a process, a process of remembering.

Think of the human brain as a building with a bunch of stories; memory is just one giant floor of this building, where many little cubicle offices reside, each harboring information about particular memories. Within each office there are file cabinets with individual folders, cradling each memory.

Experts believe that memory is not held within one part of the brain, but it involves the entire brain to recall memory. Despite the importance memory has in our everyday lives, most of this subject remains a mystery. Scientists have attempted to create computer models of the brain and its ability to remember the tiniest of details and have been very unsuccessful. You see, memories are nothing like information that can be stored on a hard drive or within the Cloud.

Memories have the potential to fade, disappear for eternity and even warp themselves into falsified information. Scientists and other brain experts have begun to attempt probing the brain on cellular levels, using optogenetic tools to manipulate neural circuits within animals. But, they are far from grasping the neural processes needed to form a full-fledged memory.

How memory works

The biological phenomenon known as encoding is the first step in the process of creating a memory. Beginning with how we perceive our world, encoding is rooted in our senses. For example, recalling the first time you met the person you first had deep feelings for involves the visual system by registering in the brain their physical features you were attracted to, like hair or eyes.

Your auditory system remembers their laugh and voice. Your smelling system may have recalled the smell of their perfume or cologne. You may even be able to recall the feeling of the ways they touched you. Each of these is separate sensations that all play a big part in the creation of one memory.

Each of these sensations goes to the hippocampus, a part of the brain that integrates each of these individual perceptions into one big picture: how you perceived and experienced the individual you fell in love with for the first time.

Scientists believe that along with the hippocampus that another key part of the brain known as the frontal cortex is responsible for the analyzing of each of those separate sensory inputs and then figuring out which ones are worth storing away to remember later. If the frontal cortex thinks that it is worth recalling, it then becomes a small part of your long-term memory that is then stored in different areas of the brain. However, how all these bits and pieces of memory are later retrieved to form a cohesive memory is yet to be discovered.

The course of storing all memories in proper ways to be later retrieved all begin with some type of perception but are all the same in the fact they are encoded and stored using the process of chemicals and electricity. Nerve cells get together with other cells at the point known as the synapse. Each action that occurs within your brain happens at the points of these synapses, where pulses of electrical power carry a message that can leap across gaps that exist between cells.

Then there is a firing of electricity across these gaps that trigger chemical messengers known as neurotransmitters. These little guys are then distributed across the spaces that lie between the cells and attach to neighboring cells. Each cell within your brain can form thousands of links, which give your brain about 100 trillion or more synapses. The areas of your brain cells that receive electrical impulses are known as dendrites and are the soft tops of the brain cells that are responsible in reaching out to neighboring brain cells.

The connections that are created between the cells in the brain are never concrete and can change at any time. In fact, they change quite frequently. All the cells within your brain work together as a network, organizing into groups that specialize in all sorts of different information processing. When one brain cell sends a signal to another, the synapse between them grows stronger. This means that the more signals that are sent between the two continue to make that connection much stronger.

As we experience new things, your brain rewires itself. Therefore, how we utilize our brains helps in the determination of how organized it is. The flexibility of our brains is known as plasticity. This kind of flexibility can help our minds to rewire itself in the chance that it ever becomes damaged.

Rapid changes to your synapses and dendrites occur as you acquire new knowledge and experience new things about the world around you. The more you experience and learn, the more connections your brain creates between various cells. Our brains are constantly organizing and reorganizing themselves in direct response to your experiences, all the while forming memories that can be triggered by outside factors.

Changes in the brain are reinforced the more you use them, giving you the ability to learn and practice newly acquired information, creating very intricate circuits of memory and knowledge that build up in the brain. For example, if you play a piece of music time and time again, this repeats the firing of certain cells many times, which is why learning that piece of sheet music becomes easier to remember over time. This makes you a better musician overtime, because of the good ole phrase of "practice makes perfect."

To encode a memory properly, you must be paying conscious attention. However, we cannot pay attention to absolutely everything. This is because our brains simply filter many things out that we encounter. If we could remember every single tiny thing each day, our brains would be on constant overload, and we would not be able to function properly. Scientists have yet to figure out how exactly we filter unimportant information out, but they do know the importance of paying attention to certain information that leads to a concrete memory.

Short-term vs. long-term memory

When a memory is created, it is always stored, even if it is only for a brief time.

There are three ways that our brains store memory:

Firstly, in the **sensory stage**

Then short-term memory

And then in **long-term memory**, but for only some recollections

These stages of storing memory act as a filter so that our brains are not flooded with too much information to adequately handle.

The start of memory creation, as you have learned, begins with a simple perception. The registration of this memory occurs in the sensory stage and typically lasts as quick as a fraction of a second. Sensory memory allows perceptions especially from our sense to linger even when the initial stimulation is over. Once the first flicker is over, this sensation is stored in our minds as a short-term memory.

Short-term memories have a limited capacity, holding about seven to maybe ten items inside our minds for a maximum of 20-30 seconds at a time. There are memory strategies that you will learn further in this book that you can practice so that you are able to hold onto short-term memories for long periods of time. Any vital information that your brain deems as important enough to keep around is then transferred from a short-term to a long-term memory. The more you repeatedly utilize this set of knowledge, the longer that this long-term memory can be retained. Long-term memory has the power to store unlimited amounts of information for indefinite amounts of time.

Many of us are particularly knowledgeable about certain sets of information, which makes it easier to recall long-term memories that are related. Therefore, individuals with average long-term memory capabilities have a great depth of information about these particular subject areas. Many people think that they have only long-term memory, but it is scientifically proven that all memories go through the sensory and short-term memory phases before it reaches the storing process that happens in the long-term memory phase.

Retrieving memories

We retrieve memories by unconsciously bringing them into our conscious mind. Many people think they have bad remembering capabilities while many individuals are quite accomplished when it comes to digging up past memories. People's brains are good at scrounging up some memories and terrible at recalling others.

If you are having issues remembering something, it is not your memory system that is to blame, but rather an inefficient component of just a single part of your memory system. If you forget something, it means that you failed to encode the information effectively – more than likely because you were distracted while the encoding process was taking place.

For example, think about how you remember where you put your eyeglasses. When you go to sleep at night, you register that you put them on your bedside table. You must be consciously aware of where you put them. Otherwise, you will not remember. When this information is successfully retained, you can then retrieve it the next morning. However, if you do not recall where you put your glasses, chances are one of a few things occurred:

You are not able to retrieve the information accurately

You failed to retain what you registered

You did not register clearly where you set them down, to begin with

If you wish to recall with better accuracy where you put your eyeglasses, then you must learn to encode in a better fashion and learn that all three stages of the remembering process must be done properly.

Or, if you have forgotten something, it may not even be that the encoding process was not done efficiently, but rather that you were distracted when the process was underway. More than likely, the exact location of where you put your glasses may have never had the opportunity to be engrained into your memory at all while encoding.

Distractions are a common deterrent when it comes to encoding memories properly. For example, if you read a business report while amongst a crowd in a bustling airport, you may think you have absorbed its information but, it was not effectively saved into your memory's hard drive for you to recall later.

Nowadays, you most likely find that there is an ever-increasing number of things that you need to remember. Therefore, you should have a decent memory. Not every person has a suitable memory - the vast majority will, in general, overlook something now and again. If so for you, you ought not to stress as there are a few different ways of memory improvement. You can discover numerous arrangements which will help you to improve your memory.

The ideal approach to this is to join every one of the accessible techniques. By doing this, you will find that you will have a higher possibility of accomplishing a more prominent degree of memory improvement. The higher the degree of progress you get, the higher the odds are of your utilizing a more significant amount of your memory.

Improvement will bring about a few points of interest. One of these preferences will be the way that you will probably retain names of the general population who you have quite recently met. This can be an extraordinary encounter, particularly for an individual who manages a lot of customers. When you have improved your memory to this level, you will have a unique possibility of giving your excellent demographic administration, and subsequently, they may move toward becoming recurrent clients.

This will prompt expanded generation in your organization. The second significant advantage of memory improvement will be that you will most likely keep substantial numbers in your memory. For consistently use, it is critical to have your distinguishing proof number, bank record number; charge card numbers, telephone numbers for your closest relative, and so forth in your mind. This is because it will be advantageous if anything sudden occurs.

A case of something unforeseen happening would be a mishap. For this situation, you might almost certainly give your rescuers the telephone numbers for your closest relative with the goal that they can be educated regarding your predicament. When you happen to be an open speaker, you can profit a great deal from memory improvement. This improvement can enable you to have the option to remember addresses in a brief span regardless of their length - so when you are approached suddenly, you can meet the challenge at hand!

Most open speakers read from or allude to discourses that are set before them - this is because they need memory improvement. A public speaker who peruses from a conversation that has been given to him/her needs memory improvement strategies. The individuals who talk structure their brains have a decent memory.

Aside from these advantages, others are related to memory improvement. You can recollect distinctively occasions that have been in the news or other media. This implies if such a theme were to emerge in a discussion, you can cite articles from papers and add to the debate because of your memory improvement. These reasons are the reason it fits for the average individual to search for memory improvement strategies.

Chapter 3: Self Testing

We realize that self-testing, which happens when understudies work on recovering information, drives learning, an associate educator of mental sciences. Under-studies can truly profit by testing themselves as they study by utilizing something as basic as cheat sheets. Notwithstanding, the key is to not drop a cheat sheet once you believe you have aced the material. Keep it as a feature of your revolution and continue rehearsing recovery of that data."

8.1 Set Goals

At the point when you set objectives for yourself, it is significant that they spur you: this implies ensuring that they are critical to you and that there is an incentive in accomplishing them. In the event that you have little enthusiasm for the result, or they are unessential given the bigger picture, at that point the odds of you placing in the work to get them going are thin. Inspiration is critical to accomplishing objectives.

Set objectives that identify with the high needs throughout your life. Without this sort of center, you can wind up with excessively numerous objectives, leaving you too brief period to commit to everyone. Objective accomplishment requires responsibility, so to boost the probability of achievement, you have to feel a desire to move quickly and have an "I should do this" frame of mind. At the point when you don't have this, you chance to put off what you have to do to make the objective reality. This thus leaves you feeling baffled and disappointed with yourself, the two of which are de-propelling. What's more, you can wind up in a damaging "I can't do anything or be effective at anything" outlook.

8.2 Develop self-Awareness

Self-awareness is having an unmistakable and reasonable impression of what your identity is. Mindfulness isn't about revealing a profound dim mystery about yourself, yet understanding what your

identity is, the reason you do what you do, how you do it, and the effect this has on others.   Self-awareness   is
 straightforwardly identified with both passionate knowledge and achievement.It encourages you to make attainable objectives since you can think about your qualities, shortcomings,

what's more, what drives you when objective setting.It enables you to manage yourself down the correct way by deciding to seek after the chances that is the best fit for your range of abilities, inclinations, and propensities.

It makes recognizing circumstances and individuals that hit our triggers and foreseeing our own responses simpler. It enables us to roll out constructive social improvements that can prompt more noteworthy individual and relational achievement Building Self-Awareness

1. Put the time in – Self-mindfulness is not learned in a book, yet accomplished through self-reflection! Use what you have found out about yourself to illuminate choices, practices, and cooperation's with

others. A few guided inquiries to kick you off:

What are 3 of your qualities and 3 of your shortcomings?

☐ What do you esteem most?
☐ What are the sentiments you are more mindful of encountering than others?
☐ What are your triggers(individuals and circumstances destined to trigger negative or awkward feelings)?
☐ How would you react under pressure?
☐ Companion, worker, competitor, and so forth.)?

2. Anticipate how you will feel and react before a circumstance and consider your real emotions and reactions after the circumstance.

3. Concentrate on your decisions - What would you be able to gain from your past triumphs and missteps? Why did you settle on a specific choice? How did this decision make you feel?

4 . Request input – self Awareness is as much about recognizing what regardless you have to learn all things considered about recognizing your qualities.

32

Requesting input on your exhibition,conduct, cooperations, can serve to improve your future activities and reactions. Input can likewise recognize parts of your conduct you aren't seeing obviously (your vulnerable sides).

5. Record (keep a diary) – Allows you to consider every day contemplations, emotions, observations, decisions, practices, and connections with others. Be straightforward with yourself. Thinking about your encounters enables you to get the hang of something that can direct your self-awareness so consider it and record it!

6. Mark your feelings – Feelings can be communicated utilizing single word, however are frequently held back. Utilize the beneath Inventory of Feelings to work on naming what you involvement with various circumstances consistently. Your emotions give knowledge into your contemplations and activities, just as enable us to more readily relate with others. You may likewise perceive slants in how you are feeling which can show you something yourself.

8.3 Reflect on what you've learned
Guidelines: when you get input from pursuers, pause for a minute to ponder the idea of any issues your pursuers related to your work.
1. Time Management: (for extra data, see Managing)
Did you deal with your time well? What would you be able to do to improve your time on the board?
2. Reason: (for extra data, see Consider Your Purpose)
Is it safe to say that you were ready to remain concentrated on one point or did your work meander? How well would you say you are adhering to directions?
3. Crowd: (for extra data, see Consider Your Audience) Did you give the models your crowd required?
4. Persona or Tone: (for extra data, see Voice, Tone, and Persona)
What did you perusers think about your tone and persona? 5. Teaming up, Revising, and Editing: (for extra data, see Collaborating, Revising, and Editing) Did your friends assess a draft of your

34

report? Provided that this is true, did their reactions help you in an important manner?

6. Altering: Did you reliably damage any principles of Standard English? (See Grammar Resources for issues with Standard English.) What sentence structure and accentuation rules or standards would you say you are experiencing issues with?

Figure out how to utilize self-reflection and reactions from pursuers to improve your composition. Students of history and thinkers are partial to stating that the individuals who don't gain from history are destined to rehash it. This perception is similarly substantial concerning your improvement as an author. Instead of putting yourself down for causing mistakes, recollect that you are in school to learn. Concentrate on the most significant weaknesses your pursuers find in your writings and afterward work to conquer these issues later on.

The Element of Reflection

Reflecting includes analyzing how you make and addressing whether you can beat obstructions to research and composing by trying different things with new creating techniques. Reflecting includes consolidating input from pundits. Reflecting includes thinking about how you can apply what you read about composition to your very own creating forms.

The last composing movement for some, individuals includes presenting their work to customers, colleagues, or chiefs. For understudies, essential crowds will, in general, be teachers or different understudies. Regardless of whether you're composing for a teacher or a customer, analysis can regularly be agonizing, so it is justifiable that a considerable lot of us attempt to abstain from hearing or contemplating our faultfinders' remarks. All things considered, your development as an essayist is to a great extent reliant on your capacity to gain from past slipups and to improve drafts because of pursuers' remarks.

Chapter 4: Accelerated Learning

Techniques

When you try accelerated learning, you'll find that there are many things that you can do to enhance your learning experience, help you learn faster and allow you to learn anything.

For instance, some people say that you can learn things much faster and more effectively if you teach or tutor someone in something that you are also learning. This gives you a better incentive to get it right and explain it better; you'd almost be explaining it to yourself, as well. You can practice the system that we talked about in the previous chapter in short bursts. Somewhere between 30 and 45 minutes should be good enough with 20 to 30-minute brakes. This will ensure maximum study time without getting tired or annoyed. If you are responsible for someone's success, you will explain things better and you will also learn a big chunk of what you are teaching, as well.

Reading aloud to yourself is something else that you may find helpful. This can help you understand it a little better. Not only this, but it will allow you to practice reading out loud.

This also connects to another technique that you can use; applying other senses. When you read something (using the sense of sight obviously) it can get boring and it may feel like you are always doing the same thing. You could read things out loud, you could also draw and build models. There are many things that you could do to enhance your learning experience!

Writing things in your own words is also something that you could benefit from. Taking the information that someone else taught you and changing it into words that you can understand better is one of the best things that you can do when you are trying to figure out how to learn something. When you have the opportunity to rewrite something or change it so that you can understand it a little better, go for it; you could benefit from it so much more than you think.

Tap into the 80/20 principle. When you are practicing accelerated learning, you are urged to try the 80/20 principle which states that 80% of your success comes from 20% of your work. So, the idea is to not waste your time on the other 80% of the work, because it isn't even important! This will save you a lot of time, helping you manage your time a lot better than before. Another really important skill that you should pick up, is the idea of blocking out distractions. Losing the phone, leaving the iPad in your bedroom, and closing out everything that you don't need on your computer are all things that you can do to help make your study experience much more effective.

You may also find it easier to study in some other places, if you find that sitting in a quiet room with the hum of the heater or air conditioner will help you focus more, you go for it. However, if you find that a noisy cafe will help you move quicker and get everything that you need to do done, then find a noisy cafe! It all really depends on your personal preferences.

Practicing is also very important when you are trying to learn new tasks; there's a reason why it is in the accelerated learning cycle! When you practice something, you exercise a part of the brain called the cerebellum. It is the part of the brain that takes care of all the movements and actions that become natural to you over time.

For example, when you were a child and you were learning how to write, you had to focus on what fingers you had to flex to actually hold the pen with a good grip. Now it comes naturally as you pick up a pen or pencil and you begin writing.

The same goes for when you are learning a new task. After practicing it for so long it just becomes embedded in your brain, and it is almost unforgettable; like riding a bike, as some say.

However, the thing is, as you start to completely learn the skill and it feels natural, you need to keep practicing it. It's like exercising. When you exercise, your body begins to feel good, you can do more and you can run faster, but if you stop running for a while, your cardio goes down. You can't run for as long as you use to. This is due to the simple fact that you have fallen out of practice. To get back into running you have to either start from square one or begin to practice again before you lose the skill completely. Keep in mind that in the early paragraph, I said "almost unforgettable."

Chapter 5: The Pleasure Of Learning- How And Why We Find Joy In Gaining Knowledge

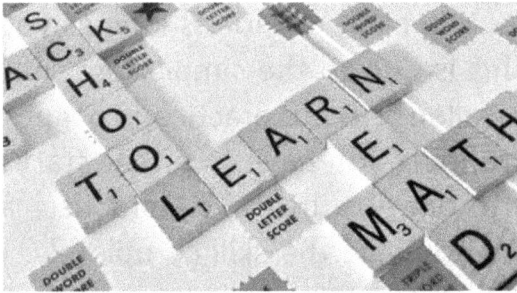

Learning is fun. Repeat that again. Learning is fun. The constant chase for knowledge drives the human race to unimaginable heights. It's taken us to the depths of the oceans and into the reaches of outer space. The human thirst for knowledge has put men on the moon, discovered millions of species alive and extinct, and keeps the bastions of higher education in business. But why? What is it about learning that gives people so much pleasure?

Biology Plays a Key Role

Humans are, at their core, competitive creatures. Tens of thousands of years ago, survival of the fittest was the law of the land. The man who could hunt the largest beast, make the sharpest spear, run the fastest and climb the highest was more likely to survive to pass his DNA to the next generation. It took skill, cunning, and innovation to live long enough to reproduce. The competition we see today in education, sport, and business stems from that early human biology.

The human race is hardwired to learn, to grow, and to advance. When we are children, we acquire new skills without a conscious thought. A baby naturally progresses from sitting, to crawling, to standing, then walking. Schoolchildren develop new skills under the watchful guidance of their teachers, and it often doesn't take long before they discover which are their favorite subjects. As adults with the freedom to follow our interests, learning never has to be a chore.

Finding Your Path to Learning

Once you've figured out your learning style, you can best decide how to make studying work for you. If you find that you're a visual learner, books and videos may be your best option. The advent of audiobooks are a boon for audible learners, and hands-on, or kinesthetic, learners may benefit from workshops or seminars.

Technology today allows for endless options at endless price points to achieve any learning goal. Libraries carry more books than ever these days and have become multimedia resources for those on a budget, offering e-books, computer access, educational programming and electronic materials. Today's libraries are a wealth of resources beyond traditional materials.

Many local colleges and cooperative extensions offer free or low-cost courses and one-day offerings. Webinars abound on nearly any subject you can think of, and can be found with a just a little online research. With such an abundance of educational opportunities, it's easier than it's ever been to find something new to learn about and find a resource to enable you to do so.

Why Does Learning Feel So Good?

Have you ever read something you need to mull over in your brain for a few moments? Then it clicks! You have a marvelous 'aha!' moment, and you can't help but smile. That 'aha!' moment has just released some endorphins, which are the human body's feel-good neurotransmitter. The more 'aha!' moments that you have, the more endorphins that will be released.

Studies show that if you are already in a good mood, and therefore releasing endorphins, **before** you begin to study, you'll actually learn faster. Activities like exercising or listening to music before studying can raise your endorphin levels and aid your learning process.

Dopamine plays a role in learning, too. This is another of the brain's 'happy' neurotransmitters. This chemical is released when you're feeling pleasure, and is kicked into high gear by being in a good mood. It's also released when you eat dark chocolate, but eating excessive amounts of sugar before studying probably isn't the best method! Maybe just one or two pieces, though…

When we feel the kick of endorphins, we're driven to want to keep that feeling alive. It's why a child doesn't want to leave a birthday party, or why we don't want a wonderful night out with friends to end. When you say, "I'm just having too much fun," what that means on a biological level is that your endorphins are high, you're feeling great, and your body doesn't want that feeling to fade.

Does this mean that the human brain can actually get addicted to learning? In a way, yes. Human beings are creatures prone to addictions, and it's proven that addiction changes the chemistry and make-up of our brains. When we hear that, we're quick to jump to the negative side of addiction. Alcohol and substance dependency can and do have ravaging effects on the makeup and function of the brain. Behavioral addictions like gambling also create these negative effects. Exercise and brain training have the opposite effect; they can build healthier brain tissue.

Is Any Addiction a GOOD Addiction?

We've all heard the term 'runner's high'. That's the effect caused by pushing the body through enough physical activity for the brain to release a surge of endorphins and dopamine. Can mental activity produce the same effect? The simple answer is yes. Pushing yourself to learn can activate the same chemicals. Once the body becomes used to these chemicals being present, it will become conditioned to want more. This is addiction, on its most basic level.

The difference between this type of addiction and addictions to unhealthy substances or behaviors comes down the effects on the brain and body. Exercise builds healthy tissue, stronger muscles, and increases the flow of oxygen to the brain. Exercise has also been shown to increase activity in the hippocampus, which is the part of the brain known to affect memory and learning. Later in this book, we will examine the hippocampus and its memory functions in depth.

Learning itself has a positive effect on the brain. The endorphins produced during those 'aha!' moments creates a desire to continue feeling good. It's shown that learning begets learning- once you've created that connection, you'll want to make the next one, and the next. In fact, the more you learn, the more you **can** learn, and you'll begin learning faster. So in a way, your own brain forms a 'good addiction' to the learning process.

Our Ever-changing Brains

On the biological level, the act of learning creates what's known as 'brain plasticity'. The brain is a constantly changing organ; it is made up of a mass of chemicals and cellular tissue and electrical activity. The healthy human brain is never stagnant, but is a nearly unimaginable number of cells in constant motion. When we learn, the brain adapts to include the new knowledge or skill. What's happening at the cellular level is that the brain is making new synaptic connections.

These connections can also help your brain build myelin, a protective material that coats the axons, or transmission cells, in the tissue. The erosion of myelin is linked to diseases which affect neurological function, most notably multiple sclerosis. The reduction of myelin also plays a role in the brain function of patients afflicted with Alzheimer's disease and Parkinson's disease.

The brain is a wondrous machine. It is a powerhouse; it's a memory vault; it's a speech center, and so much more. It's the organ that regulates the rest of our organs. If learning can increase its function and its productivity, **and** protect against potentially devastating disease, then learning should be an activity to be embraced and practiced regularly.

The Competition Factor

Early in this chapter, we briefly touched upon the innate competitive nature of humans. Why do schools depend on grading systems? Why do they hand out awards, and why do they name a valedictorian? Because it feels so good to succeed. Successful students aren't always necessarily the smartest students, but they are the ones who are willing to work hard to receive recognition. Being recognized for effort and achievement is yet another thing which releases those endorphins. In short, winning feels good, in and beyond the academic arena.

Competition in the adult world is what fuels business and innovation. Successful corporations are made up of people who are smart, savvy, and most importantly, willing to learn and adapt in a rapidly changing global economic climate. Those who cannot learn and grow will be left behind.

Scientific advances are also being made every day by people who are devoted life-long learners. Diseases are being cured, food is being engineered to feed more people, and the outer reaches of space are being explored using man-made equipment developed over centuries of discovery and experimentation. These advances wouldn't exist without people who are open to learning and those who are persistent in their pursuit of greater knowledge.

Turning Failures into Successes

One of the other joys we can take from learning is the joy of failure. Yes, that sounds counterintuitive, but failure can fuel big success. We've all heard stories of big name athletes who were cut from their high school squads, notably the inspirational tale of Michael Jordan being cut from his varsity basketball team. He really showed them, huh?

People who can learn from their failures are people who can analyze what went wrong, and turn the situation around into something that goes wildly right. By learning what their weakness was, finding a solution to improve upon it, and using that knowledge to become first proficient and then superior in those skills, failure is turned into success.

Approaching perceived failure as a learning tool is a healthy way to keep yourself motivated. It goes back to that ingrained need for competition, and sometimes the person we need to compete with the most is our self. Integrating the self-reflection discussed in the first chapter with the biological factors covered in this one is a great way to get on the road to meeting your learning goals.

Another way you can take your learning to the next level is by eating foods that have a positive effect on your brain health. In the next chapter, we'll take a look at some of the food groups that have the most benefit for your brain and how to incorporate them into your diet.

Chapter 6: Why Does Memory Fail?

What is "forgetting"?

When it is not in the grip of some pathology, the human brain is capable of storing LTMs permanently, however "memory decay" is regarded as a normal physiological process. If new neural connections can easily be made then, by the same token, old ones that haven't been used in a while can be lost by the brain's natural "pruning" mechanism. Forgetting can also be the result of poor initial encoding or faulty information retrieval. Forgetting tends to occur quickly at first, but then slows as time progresses.

There are four key reasons why your memory sometimes fails.

Lack of attention – Attention is the cornerstone of learning and memory: if we don't pay proper attention to things, we are not going to store them, it's really as simple as that. The mind is most susceptible to lack of attention during moments of "vagueness", which is something that most of us have experienced from time to time. For example, you take your car to drive out to a friend's house but half-way there it suddenly dawns on you that you're heading in the direction of your family member's house instead! And all because they live along a more familiar route which you have become habituated to. This is a classic example of vagueness and wandering attention.

Disuse and the passage of the time – Memories will weaken and decay when not in active use (this is the principle that lies behind that old saying "use it, or lose it!") Nothing is forever, even when long-term memory is concerned, if you don't occasionally access stored information. Also, whenever you are forming brand new LTMs you are sometimes creating amnesia for those LTMs already in storage when they are seldom accessed or used. You might experience this when, in adult life, you try to access certain rote-learned mathematical formulas that you knew in childhood and find that you can't summon forth the information. This is because the original data has decayed due to underuse or non-use.

Interference patterns caused by older memories – There are sometimes occasions when we are trying to learn something new, that old bits of learned information will effectively compete with the new data and cause interference in the learning process. This is especially so when the new and old information are similar to each other. Scientists call this "proactive inhibition". A good example of this is learning to drive on the right-hand side of the road (as in the United States or on the European continent) when you are already habituated to driving on the left-hand side of the road, as in Great Britain. It can also occur when you are trying to master the functions on a brand new mobile phone yet the memory of how to operate the previous model that you owned is interfering with this learning process.

One's emotional state – All experiences that have an emotional charge are remembered with ease. This is due to hormonal and chemical discharges in the brain such as adrenalin and cortisol, the so-called "stress hormones". And yet, having said this, negatively charged emotions tend to be forgotten over time due to the brain's natural defense mechanism by which is clears out harmful and damaging content. Paradoxically, this phenomenon known as "motivated forgetting", by which we actively participate in the oblivion of certain kinds of events (especially those of a traumatic or disturbing nature), helps us to prevent or minimize the negative emotional impact they may have on us. This process can interfere with the formation and retention of memories.

The above may be condensed into a further four general principles governing why memory often fails us:

·Failure in registration or codification – These failures are usually due to a failure of attention, or insufficient investment of attention, sometimes due to our having been distracted. This is because we were not sufficiently motivated or interested in the information, or perhaps we were simply engrossed in our own thoughts.

·Little or poor understanding of what is retained – This can happen when you read some text in a passive or superficial way, without actively thinking about the implications of what you are reading.

·Failure in the memory storage processes – This can happen when you fail to make timely memory reviews of acquired information, or when you've accumulated too much information for the memory to assimilate everything at once.

·Failure in the processes of evocation – Sometimes, when the information is stored in our memory, we experience a failure in the evocation or recovery of the aforementioned information. This is a simple failure in memory-retrieval processes.

Chapter 7: Ways To Learn Effectively

In order to start down the road toward the accomplishment of your goals you must first learn how to effectively pick up information in a more successful fashion. While there are various trains of thought in terms of making this possible for you, there are some specific strategies you should pay close attention to if you are dedicated to making this a reality for you. Here are the best ways for you to start learning things even faster and more effectively.

Pay Attention to the Way That You Learn

Everyone learns things in a different way. Some people are visual learners, some are written learners and others learn by doing or even by hearing information. The only way for you to become an effective learner and to become more successful is to make sure that you are aware of the best way for you to learn the things set in front of you. Remember everybody is different and what works for someone else should be irrelevant to you. Experimentation is key, see what works for your own individual needs!

Get Rid of Distractions

Make sure that you create an environment that fosters learning. When you want to take information in, you need to make sure that you are devoting your full attention to the matter at hand. Turn off your phone, turn off the radio and give everything to what you are learning. As it is, your daily life is filled with too many distractions and things that try to get in the way of your tasks, however, now is the time to take as many as possible out of your way. One more thing, turn off the social media. Yes I am talking about the facebook, twitter, chapsnap, instagram, and the list goes on and on! It is amazing how much better and faster you can learn when you are 100% focused on the task at hand.

Take Notes

Not only does it help to remove distractions, it's also beneficial for you to get into the habit of making notes for yourself. Not only can it help to write things down, but you should consider making voice recordings, as well if you can process information easier in that way. In addition, this will give you twice the reinforcement for your information to make it stick better. I have found from my own personal experience that writing information down, in note form, which helps me to remember and learn upwards to 200% more! Don't down play how crucial taking notes can, this is a huge mistake!

Be Able To Explain To Others

When you go through the information in front of you, try to look at it in terms of being able to teach someone else what you have learned. If you approach things in this manner then you should be able to see the material in a different light.

If you feel that you have learned something completely than you will easily feel comfortable that you can explain it to anyone else. Once you begin to feel this may, go a step further, and try to explain it to somebody. Even if you are too scared to do this in the physical form, you could easily sign into Skype, find a random person in a random online forum, and attempt teaching them. This may sound crazy but it works! The smartest and best learners in this world are teachers, become one if you want to step up your learning game!

Ask Questions to Test Your Knowledge

It may sound like crazy advice, but talk to yourself about what you are learning. Ask yourself questions to make sure that you are grasping the knowledge that you are working on permanently absorbing. If you can't answer them randomly, then you need to look at it from another perspective. The point is to actually take the information in completely and not just memorize facts so that you completely understand the subject matter. I have found that being able to answer questions that I ask myself has allowed me to retain information I have learned for much longer periods of time.

Relate the Material to Your Life

For you to truly understand the material deep down, you have to make a connection to it. Find a way to relate your subject matter to your life in some way to make sure that it has firmly become your knowledge. This may seem difficult if you are learning something that is completely out of your element, but if you can find a way to somehow tie it all in, even if you are the only one that sees the connection, then you will master it.

Fake it until you make it

One of the greatest secrets to learning faster, processing information more effectively, and attaining knowledge for longer periods of time is the strategy of faking it until you make it.

What I mean by this is to pretend that you have already learned the information in 100% perfect fashion. Pretend that you love the material you are learning, even if you don't. Pretend, or fake, that you are the greatest learner in the whole entire world, even if your grades have not indicated it.

Fake it until you make it can change your life. There have been countless tests and studies run that the brain cannot distinguish between what you perceive to be real or fake. The most important thing is controlling the way you think. If your thoughts are positive, and are in alignment with your goals, you will have a much better chance of learning the material in comparison to being negative, doubtful, and unsure of your abilities.

Chapter 8: The Interview Process

The first step in landing any job knows your qualifications. If you want to be a Rocket Scientist, it would be best to know and understand what qualifications will be required. One way to do this is by looking at job postings for the job you are chasing and comparing your personal resume with what is being asked. For the sake of this book we will assume you have all of the qualifications for the position and we will move on to the interview process.

Every candidate will need a concise resume and cover letter written specifically for the position for which they are applying. Ensure with every cover letter the specific company and exact position title are addressed and even if your qualifications exceed a one page resume, it is best to try and keep your credentials to no longer than two pages. The best would be one page. Often, overly large and elaborate resumes will deter potential employers as the human resources department will often vet through the applications prior looking for ones which are not well written, poorly organized or overly lengthy.

If you are able, having an online resume to expand on your shorter, more concise application, will aid those who have furthered interest in your capabilities to view your longer and more detailed credentials. Including your personal mission statement and any keywords often used to describe the position, within your resume and cover letter is another helpful way to show the hiring committee you share the same values. Often, hiring committees will weed out applications, which do not include these items.

Now that your resume and cover letter are primed and set for success, you are onto the next step, which is going through the interview process. Each company will conduct their interviews in a slightly different manner but there will always be key elements which remain the same. Weather your interview is over the phone or in person you may be required to interview for the position more than once.

It is also important to remember that every interview process will be a little different because every company and every interviewer is different. Every interviewer has their own perspective and ideas which they feel are most important for the position they are hiring. If the person conducting the interview is the person who will also be your boss they may have their own ideas about how their team will best function which will ultimately lead to different types of questions and different types of details they would like from you.

It is important to prepare for a variety of questions and variations of those questions so you are capable of answering each question quickly with efficiency and attention to detail. It could also be that the interviewer will simply use text book questions and not attempt to customize the interview process.

Depending on the industry for which you are applying questions can be more technical, behavioral, or even specific to the job or field of work. While it is difficult to say exactly how an interview will be performed we can do our best to break down the basics of the interview process and give you a good idea of what to expect. Do your best to impress your interviewer and convince them of your fit with the company within the first five minutes. Studies have shown that interviewers make up their mind about a candidate within the first five minutes and the rest of the interview is just confirmation about their decision. Those first five minutes are crucial. Come into the room with high energy and enthusiasm and make sure to tell them how appreciative you are of the interview. Remember that you may not be the only person interviewed that day and depending on what number in line you are, the interviewer may be tired and feel as though they have been playing a broken record with the same answers the entire day. You want them to remember you. Start out with a positive comment such as

"I have really been looking forward to this interview and meeting you. I think your company is doing great work and I am excited by the idea of becoming part of the team."

Interviewers often view interviews as adversarial. It can seem as though candidates are trying to pry a job offer out of the interviewer. The interviewer's job is to hold on to that offer until they are convinced by the interviewees pitch for the job. You need to transform the tug of war dynamic into a relationship where you are on the same side as your interviewer.

Begin by opening with kind words about the company and stating how happy you are to learn more about the company from someone who currently works there and provide some background information about yourself so you can figure out if this will be a good fit. Stating that you always think it is unfortunate to hire someone who turns out to not be a good match making no one happy will gain you some points with the interviewer for sure.

Chapter 9: Understanding The Human

Brain

Our body consists of different organs that are crucial to our survival and wellbeing; every organ and system comprised of different organs plays an important role in our proper functioning.

The human brain and the nervous system are undoubtedly the most important bodily organs and systems. Your brain and nervous system are directly involved in learning and memory retention; it is therefore important that to train your brain, you have a firmer understanding of how the brain works. Let us learn how the brain works:

How the Brain Works

Your brain functions like a huge, complex computer system that has the capability to run several functions simultaneously. It processes all the information it receives from your body and senses, decodes the message and then responds to them by sending different signals to your body. You think, experience emotions, analyze things, plan stuff, and make decisions because the brain is doing its job and working correctly.

The human brain looks like an oversized walnut that has scores of crevices and folds that collectively have around 100 billion neurons and a trillion supporting cells that stabilize the tissue.

While the brain has various regions, the prominent ones include the cerebrum, cerebellum, the diencephalon comprising of pituitary gland, hypothalamus and thalamus, and the brain stem comprising of midbrain, medulla, and pons.

The cerebrum has two halves known as the right and left hemispheres. These two halves connect via the corpus callosum, a thin bundle comprising of nerve fibers. Each of the two hemispheres has six lobes in charge of carrying out different functions.

Your cerebrum processes sensory information and controls your bodily movements. The cerebrum is also the birthplace of all unconscious and conscious feelings, thoughts, and actions. The cerebrum also controls your hearing, memory, intelligence, and speech.

The functions of your left and right hemispheres are diverse and dissimilar. The left hemisphere is in charge of abstract thinking and speech whereas the right hemisphere is responsible for imagery and spatial thinking. The right side of your brain controls your body's left side whereas the left side of your brain controls the right side of your body. Any damage to your brain's left hemisphere can result in paralysis of the right side of your body whereas damage to your brain's right hemisphere can paralyze the left side of your body.

Your left cerebral cortex is in charge of your language and speech while the right cerebral cortex provides spatial information such as how your hand is moving right now. Your thalamus supplies your cerebrum with sensory information received from your ears, eyes, and skin (all the senses really). Your hypothalamus is in charge of regulating your sleep, thirst and hunger, and together with the pituitary gland, it also manages the production of various hormones within your body.

The brain stem is in charge of relaying information between the spinal cord, cerebellum, and brain. It additionally controls facial expressions and eye movements, and regulates functions such as your heartbeat, blood pressure, and breathing. Your cerebellum coordinates different bodily movements, and is in charge of maintaining balance.

How Memory and Memory Retention Works

To have a better understanding of how memory and memory retention works, it is first important to understand the types of memory and how the different stages of memory work. We have two main types of memory: short-term and long-term memory.

Short-Term Memory

Your short-term memory closely relates to your working memory, which is why use of the two terms is often interchangeable.

We call it short-term memory because by nature, this is memory stored in your mind for a very small amount of time. During this short period, the brain decides whether to turn the memory into long-term memory or discard it altogether. It can last anywhere from 15 to 30 seconds, and serves as the Random-access memory (RAM) of your brain. This means your short-term memory is home to the information you are using in the present as you work on, or actively engage in something. Any new information you gather using your five senses is 'short-term memory' until the brain decides whether to commit it to your long-term memory

Long-Term Memory

Your long-term memory is the organized system of your brain that is in charge of storing information, sorting it out, managing all the information, and then retrieving the required piece of information when needed.

Long-term memory further divides into the following pillars:

1: Explicit Memory

Also called declarative memory, this type of long-term memory requires you to think consciously. For example, if you consciously think of the first time you drove a bicycle at the age of 7, you will recall an explicit memory. Explicit memory further splits into two more types: episodic and semantic memories.

Episodic memory signifies the memories you build related to any important events, instances, and episodes in your life. For instance, recalling the time your partner proposed to you is an apt example of episodic memory. Semantic memory, on the other hand, refers to the memory related to any concept, fact, or idea learned. For example, your knowledge of the Krebb's cycle is an example of semantic memory.

2: Implicit Memory

With this kind of long-term memory, you do not need conscious recall of something because once a memory becomes an implicit memory; it means the memory has become a part of your autopilot program. For example, if for the last seven years you have been drinking a glass of water immediately after waking up each morning, you are likely to wake up and unconsciously reach for the glass of water on your nightstand so that you can drink some water. Implicit memory also comprises of procedural memory that signifies the memory related to any skills, tasks, or talents you have attained over time.

Now that you are aware of the different types of memories, let us look at how we create memories.

The Memory Formation Process

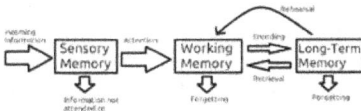

Image courtesy of wiki commons

The memory formation process comprises of different steps through which you pick up information and then turn it into your long-term memory depending on the personal importance you attach to the information gathered.

Since you are already aware of the steps involved in the process, here, we shall aim to cultivate a deeper understanding of the steps and processes:

1: Memory Acquisition/Memory Encoding

This step/process involves data gathering and acquisition. Every time you learn anything or distill new information, it creates a temporary neural pathway in the brain. The type and nature of the information determines the particular location of the pathway. For example, if you are reading a map, the neurons in your right parietal lobe of the brain will be active as this lobe is in charge of processing and saving spatial information.

When you pick up a piece of information, the brain immediately stores it in your short-term memory because at that very instant, it is yet to determine the importance of the information collected and whether it should store or discard it.

Oftentimes, the information you gather or notice fades away if you do not commit it to your long-term memory. To ensure information does not fade away, all there is to do is ensure that the brain successfully encodes the information. This is a complicated process that begins with perceiving some information aka stimulus through any one or more of your five senses.

The different kinds of encoding include tactile (when information related to your sense of touch is encoded), semantic (when information related to sensory data required in a particular context is encoded), acoustic (when auditory input such as sounds, words, and noises are encoded) and visual (when information related to your visual sense is encoded.)

To ensure the brain commits a short-term memory to your long-term memory, the brain has to successfully encode this information. One surefire way to do that is to focus on the information you want to encode. Once encoded, the memory consolidation stage starts.

2: Memory Consolidation

Memory consolidation refers to the process of strengthening your neuronal pathways so that the brain encodes a certain piece of information and moves it from short-term to long-term memory.

Scientists are yet to understand this process in its entirety, but what we know for sure is that the process involves several factors. The most notable of these factors are your emotional involvement with a certain memory and your level of focus on it. For instance, if you are highly focused on a task, your brain will properly encode and consolidate every piece of information related to it and then turn it into long-term memory.

Another factor involved in the process is the existence of any similar neuronal pathways. If there is any other already-formed memory stored in your brain related to the new piece of information you are trying to memorize, you will establish the nexus between the two and consolidate the memory quickly. If you are learning how to cook curry, for example, and you have made a sauce similar to it before, you are likely to memorize the new recipe quickly.

3: Memory Retrieval

This is the final stage of the memory formation process; this stage occurs when you wish to recall some information committed to your consolidated memory.

Our brains retrieve all consolidated memories using the specific and unique neuronal pathways it stores them in. When you think of some information committed to your long-term memory, its neuronal pathway becomes active; instantaneously after stimulation, you successfully retrieve that piece of information.

It is easier and quicker to activate neuronal pathways that you have properly strengthened and focused on over time. For instance, the process through which you submit a visa application for Europe may be committed to your long-term memory, but if you have not recalled it in 6 months, it may take a while to retrieve that information. On the other hand, it will take you a fraction of second to recall the lyrics of a song you sing day in and day out.

To quickly learn, memorize, and retrieve things, you need to work on all the stages of the memory formation process elaborated above. The process starts with the acquisition of a certain piece of information that the brain then encodes so that it can then move on to the consolidation process. Only by consolidation can our brains effectively turn information into long-term memory. You then need to recall that information repeatedly and involve yourself emotionally in the experience to retrieve it instantly every time you need that information.

If you often experience trouble retrieving information on time, it is likely you are experiencing certain problems that obstruct your focus and hamper your ability to consolidate a memory. The next chapter talks about the different causes of low memory retention.

Chapter 10: Tools That Help With

Accelerated Learning

Accelerated Learning
Accelerated learning is revolutionary. It is the key to the future and what has helped us get so far in such a short space of time. Accelerated learning involves putting an individual or a business through a more rigorous and effective course than what a mainstream class would offer you, in order to learn at a quicker and more efficient rate, which in turn, allows you to learn a lot more in a shorter space of time. The great things about accelerated learning is that it offers an individual an environment that encourages them to thrive. In many mainstream classes, often the environment will discourage those individuals that excel, simply because society enjoys bringing people down. Accelerated learning puts an individual around passionate people who truly care about the quality at which the individual is

learning and being taught. Here are a few tools that help accelerate the rate of learning.

Putting what you Learn into Practice

Perhaps this is the most important tool and piece of knowledge to remember when wanting to learn at an accelerated pace. It is simply not enough to simply have information thrown at you. This is an unfair expectation to have simply because the mind doesn't always retain everything that you ever come across or are taught. Putting what you have learnt into action helps the mind retain it easier. For example, it is more likely someone will remember a time in history if they make a little play on it.

Use your Senses

It may seem like common sense, but one of the best ways to accelerate the rate at which you learn is to learn about something by introducing the topic to all of your senses. Your mind is more likely to remember something when many different aspects of you can relate to it.

This is why you feel such a strong connection to someone who you've experienced a lot of things with, they have interacted with the majority of your senses.

Questions

Asking questions is definitely an underappreciated tool in this day and age. It is disheartening how people are so quick to judge someone if they ask a question that may seem obvious. The fact of the matter is, every question is a great question. How can you expect to learn at a quick pace if you don't actually ask a question? Asking the right question can accelerate your learning exponentially, so make sure that you are always asking a question if you are unsure about something.

Chapter 11: Accelerated Learning Can

Change Your Life

What is Accelerated Learning?

Accelerated learning is a type of learning that helps an individual excel in whatever they are trying to learn. Obviously, accelerated learning offers a much more vigorous program compared to mainstream learning, but the benefits that you gain from it greatly outweigh the downsides. The key aspect of accelerated learning is that it is accelerated. It's all about learning quickly rather than slowly and thoroughly. Of course, an individual doesn't get the same thorough learning experience, but they are still offered exactly the same learning content, but just in a different way.

Accelerated Learning Vs Mainstream Learning

Mainstream Learning

Mainstream classes are offered to the majority of the educated populace. The upside to these type of classes is that students and individuals are offered a thorough learning course. The key difference between accelerate classes and mainstream classes is the time-frame individuals are given to learn a subject. The downsides to mainstream classes is that the quality of learning is much lower than accelerate classes. This is because there is generally more students in the mainstream classes, and these students as well as the students aren't as locked in as students and teachers that are in accelerated classes.

Accelerate Learning

Accelerate learning is generally offered to students and individuals that excel in mainstream classes. It gives these individuals the opportunity to apply themselves without having to worry about the distractions that are offered from mainstream classes. Of course, accelerate learning is much more stressful than mainstream learning, but this is only because people that are in accelerate classes take their education much more serious than the majority of people in mainstream classes. Accelerate learning offers an individual everything that they'd learn from a mainstream class, but at a much quicker rate and they are also offered other aspects of a subject also. It is for people who are willing to go the extra mile.

Accelerate Learning is the Best way to Learning

It is no secret that accelerate learning is the best way to learn. The best part about accelerate learning and accelerate classes is that people are passionate about your learning and learning in general. The environment is a perfect one to be in if you are searching for a place to learn without the distractions that mainstream learning offers an individual. Of course, it is stressful to be in an accelerate class, but it is much better to be stressing over the work instead of stressing over actually getting work or people not caring at all about your education. Accelerate learning is the future.

Chapter 12. Physical Prerequisites For Learning - Create Your Personal Learning Environment

" Education does not come from reading, but from thinking about what is read. "(Carl Hilty)

A) The learning environment

In order to make the most efficient use of the time spent on learning, it is important to create an **environment** in which **the risk of being distracted is minimized** . Especially when you want to learn to spend the evening in the evenings, you push the many small things that still have to be done. Household, shopping, telephone, internet, the evening television program, friends. Determine for themselves **when** they are devoting themselves to which occupation and, if possible, stick to it. **When they learn, they learn, nothing else.**

The right place to learn

Think about it, too, where can you probably learn the most undisturbed:

· Is the living room really the right place?

· Do you have the possibility to set up in their home office without being permanently disturbed?

· Or is the walk into the local library the more worthwhile way?

Psycho-psychologically it is useful to **always choose the same place,** to arrange it so that you can start directly **without having to set up a long time** and adjust the environment, eg by switching off the cell phone, the flatmate is to understand that you at this time DO Not want to be disturbed and other things.

The right time to learn

Just as important as the right place is **the right time** to learn. As we know, we are more receptive and productive in the morning than in the afternoon. In general it is often difficult in the evening to focus the last resources left over from the day to learning. But there are also enough people who are able to work through whole nights productively. Also you can get used **to the place and time** . When you put **routine** into an action, it often takes only a few weeks to get used to it, and **a new habit has been** established.

Find out for yourself what kind of **location and time** they are and try to adapt their **learning units** . It makes little sense to learn late every night if they did not keep them from it the next morning. The time could then use them differently.

Also, note that learning is not equal learning and consists of different activities. Getting a whole new area needs more attention and strength than reading a text again. Completing an exercise requires more energy than the next stack of cards.

B) External factors - Avoid stress and pressure

So that it does not come so far that external influences such as pressure, expectation, etc., affect their psyche, they should counteract possible sources **early** . Keep an eye on the available time so as not to fall under time pressure. If colleagues, supervisors, acquaintances tend to ask them permanently how they are studying and they are also struggling, they introduce clear rules. Tell them courteously, but definitely, that they let themselves know at their own time how they are going. Your fellow human beings will certainly understand this.

But also from the lecturers and fellow students, they should not be subjected to psychological negative pressure.**Please clarify** the requirements for an examination **in advance in order** to be able to prepare yourself adequately and do not ask the lecturer two days beforehand. In particular, as far as house and holiday work and project work are concerned, they are informed of all formal requirements at an early stage, they receive feedback in due time and clarify questions as soon as they arise. This prevents them from being overwhelmed by problems, questions and other requirements and uncertainties, and that they affect the quality of their work.

C) Learning material - the working tool

Depending on the university, study subject and lecturers, there is today a huge arsenal of information sources. The classic textbook covers only a small part of the possibilities. In the multimedia age, lectures are recorded and can be called up at any time on the Internet. Audio books and podcasts are becoming more and more popular, which is why the supply is steadily increasing. Commercial repetitors offer private tutoring lessons and online courses are offered by both university and civilian institutions. You can still write the protected card types yourself, or use an app on the smartphone to pick them up and repeat them after generated time intervals.

The offer is almost unmanageable. It is all the more important that they find out at an **early stage which materials and in which form are best suited for them** . Here is the simple rule: Trying is about studying. This means:

· Look at the possibilities offered by their university and how they are crammed with their learning materials and access sources

· Take the time and look for a library or bookstore and get an overview of the possibilities in printed form

· Textbooks are often comprehensive and go into the depth of a topic scripts, on the other hand, are compact and therefore offer a good start to a topic

· In some study courses there are also study commentaries dealing with the main aspects of the examination

· Examinations for practicing with sample answers

· Question-answer books to query and verify the learned knowledge

· Map types can be found at almost every course of study.

Weigh the advantages and disadvantages of the various utensils and literature. Choose between time and benefits.Thus, ready - printed card types are quite practical. However, the learning effect of creating the cards itself is also an unspeakable advantage. Think of the above as well as passive and active learning. Listening to an audio book, speaks different channels and has other prospects for success than writing questions, sketching and solving problems. If they find the perfect mixture that is **optimally adapted to their learning type** , they learn more efficiently, ie, more successfully, at the same time.

TIP : Do not underestimate the importance of the right learning environment. Learn in a quiet place - always the same and at the same   time.
Avoid   being   distracted.
Invest time in a good preparation for learning by dealing with all available materials and finding the best for them.

Chapter 13: Speed Reading Techniques

Whether you are analyzing a Shakespearean play for your literature class or you are browsing a material that you will need to learn later, reading could be tedious for some. Speed reading could be a strategy, which can help you learn much faster. It is true that reading faster could result to less learning. But through practice, you can combat this effect.

Avoid Subvocalizing

Probably you have realized that when you read, you are subvocalizing or moving your mouth as you try to speak the words to yourself. This habit could help you recall some concepts, but it could also be a primary barrier to faster learning. An easy way to fight this habit is to chew gum while you are reading. This will occupy the muscles that are mainly used for subvocalizing.

Avoid Reading Words that You Have Already Read

If you are reading, your eyes have the tendency to move back to previous words. More often than not, these are brief movements that will not help you to enhance your memory. You can use an index card to cover words after reading them. This habit also happen if you have failed to understand the words that you are reading. If your eyes are jumping several lines back, this is an indicator that you should start slowing down.

Take Note of Your Eye Movements

Once you are reading, the eyes may move erratically, skipping some words and pausing on other. Take note that you can only effectively read if your eyes are steady. If you try to make less movements for every line, you can read a lot faster. But you must be cautious. Recent studies suggest limits to how you can read at once:

The human eye can read only 4 letters to the left of your eye position, but 8 letters to the right. On average, this is about 2 to 3 words at once.

You can see letters about nine to 15 spaces to the right of your eyes. However, you can't read them.

Regular readers cannot process words on the other lines. Practicing fast reading by skipping lines while still understanding them could be a real challenge.

Practice Your Eyes to Make Less Movements

Research reveals that the human brain can decide where to focus our eyes according to how long or familiar the next words look like. You will be able to read faster if you practice your eyes to move to certain areas on the page. Below is an an exercise that you can try:

Put an index card over a text line.

On the card, write an X over the first word. On the same line, write another X. Put three words further for clear understanding, 5 words for basic texts, or seven words if you want only to browse the primary points.

Until you reach the end of the line, place more X within similar spacing.

Read fast as you slide down the index card, exerting effort to only pay attention to the word just under every X.

Aim for a Faster Pace, Which You Could Understand

There are speed reading programs that promises to increase your reading pace by harnessing first your reflexes, then practicing until your brain could catch up. But take note that this has not been established as a proven strategy first. It may help you increase the speed you move through the material. However, the level of understanding may not be enough. If you want extreme speed reading, you can try the exercise below:

Use a pen or a pencil to move along the text. Take note of the time and complete just as you reach the end of the line.

Start by reading for a minute following the pace of the pen. Do this even if you can't understanding what you are reading. Keep your focus on the text and just move your eyes for the whole minute.

Rest for at least 30 seconds, then aim for a faster pace.

Text Skimming

You can use skimming to gain a basic understanding of the material that you want to study. Skimming can be used to learn crucial concepts out of a textbook to prepare for an exam. Take note that skimming is not a good alternative if you need comprehensive reading.

Read Headings and Titles

Start by only reading the chapter titles and subheadings at the beginning of main sections.

Read the Start and End of a Section

Textbook usually contain summaries and introductions of every chapter. You can read the start and end paragraph of an article or a chapter. If you are familiar with the subject, you can quickly read. However, don't try to speed read extremely. You can save time by skipping most of the paragraphs, but it is more important to learn what you are reading.

Highlight Important Terms throughout the Material

If you want to learn fast, run your eyes quickly across the material instead of your normal reading pace. After reading the gist of the text, you can select keywords, which mark significant areas. Pause and highlight the following terms:

Terms that are repeated several times

The primary concepts – usually involving terms from the section headings or titles

Proper nouns

Words that are italicized, in bold letters or underlined

Words that you don't know the meaning

Analyze Diagrams and Pictures

The accompanying diagrams and pictures usually present a lot of information without too much reading needed. Exert extra effort to make certain that you understand the message of every diagram.

If You Are Confused, Read the First Sentence of Every Paragraph

If you have lost track of the concept, you can read the start of every paragraph. More often than not, the first two sentences will refresh you of the crucial points.

Learn the Material through Your Annotations

Return to the words that you have highlighted. Can you understand these words and obtain a general idea of what the material is all about? If you are confused at a specific word, you can try to read several sentences that are surrounding the word to remind yourself of the subject. Highlight added words as you run this.

 Exercise

Keep track of your progress by timing the speed of your reading. Try to beat your speed so you can stay motivated. Try the exercise below so you can time your reading in WPM or Words Per Minute.

Count the number of words in one line and multiply it by the number of lines on one page

Set a timer for five minutes and measure how much lines you could read in that timeframe

Multiply the number of words per page by the number of pages you read. Divide the answer by five to obtain your estimated WPM.

There are also online test to measure your WPM, but you might read at a different speed on a printed page than on a screen.

Your reading pace must improve if you practice these exercises regularly. You can even double your reading speed after several weeks. Establish your milestones to encourage yourself to improve your speed.

200 to 250 WPM is ideal for 12 years old and above

300 WPM is ideal for college students

450 WPM is ideal if you are student skimming for primary concepts

1000 WPM is considered a competitive speed.

Remember, understanding the concept is more important than achieving a record speed.

Chapter 14: A Few Other Techniques

In this day and age there are far too many distractions available to take our attention away from the tasks at hand. But if you would like to be able to memorize information faster and become a better learner there are a few techniques you can employ to help you double or even triple the amount of information you can retain in your sessions. When you allow yourself to be distracted you make it that much harder for your brain to simple take in the information you are presenting it. With those other distractions joking for the position of attention in your mind it will force you to work that much harder to try and remember.

If you are a music lover try to listen to music without lyrics. Music with lyrics can interfere with your language processing abilities. So when you listen to music with lots of lyrics you're essentially sabotaging yourself. Your brain will be unable to totally focus on one set of information because the other will either be spoken or read and disrupt the flow of the other. So instead try to listen to music that is only instrumental. If you can stay away from music that has any lyrics your can still listen to sounds in the background without distracting yourself from the material and make learning and retention that much easier.

Try to choose times that are most conducive to studying. If you choose to work when you are very likely to be interrupted, you will easily be distracted with each interruption and make it that much harder for yourself. Also shoot for times with your have energy. If you are tired your mind is likely to be clear and able to engage in the types of mental gymnastics you are asking of it. You would never ask you body to run a marathon when you are exhausted so why ask the same of your brain? It is a muscle too. By keeping distractions to a minimum and being properly energized you are also less likely to experience stress while studying which can also make it easier on yourself. The more stressed you are the harder it will be to concentrate on the task at hand.

With the technology available to us it can be extremely hard to disconnect from everything and everyone around us. By having a cellphone, you are totally accessible to everyone at all times. This constant connection can be so distracting, talking with your friends or finding out what someone just posted on Facebook can be so much more engaging then the studying you are trying to accomplish. But if you want to be able to memorize and retain the information you are working with you need to do yourself a favor and unplug from everything around you. Turn off notifications, your cell phone, whatever you need to do to be totally focused on the task at hand. This can be very hard for some people especially if they have never done it before. If this is the case for you try for about 20 minutes at a time. You don't want to drive yourself to distraction by being unplugged because that wont achieve anything either.

Many people studying sitting or laying down. While this restful state can help keep you focused on one thing and one thing only you also don't want to completely sit like a lump the whole time. Standing and walking around for short breaks can help promote blood flow and even energy into your body. Both are helpful for keeping you fresh and focused. You also provide more oxygen to your brain from the increased blood flow and the more oxygen your brain has the better it will function.

Prioritize the material you are about to review. If say you feel very confident on certain parts of the information you are cover then you should skip those parts and review what you are shakier with. When you go over material you are already very familiar with you can give yourself a false sense of security. You will feel like you know more and take time away from the information that really needs your attention. It will also increase your exposure to what you are unfamiliar with helping you to each maximum retention of all the topics you are trying to remember.

Tell yourself a story. This is one that can't be stressed enough, if you can find a story to help show you the information you are trying to learn that's excellent and you should read it. But if you can make one up, by placing information into a relatable story your brain will have an easier time remember that then trying to chock down random bits of information. Telling your story to someone else or even attempting to teach them material will also help you to better retain it. When you teach someone else you are forced to reword the information and put it into each to understand bites for someone who doesn't know the material. This rewording and forcing you to really work with the concepts will give you a better understanding and make it that much easier to understand.

The last tip to keep in mind is to try and preview the content you are about to go over. By going on other websites or searching in other books before getting down to some serious studying or memorization you can help to give yourself perspective on material that might not necessarily be clear from the source you are currently reading. It can make things clearer it can also give you different perspective that can help the information to click in your mind and help you to remember it better. You can also give yourself a bigger picture if you skim before you read in detail. You will better be able to see where the text is heading and hopefully by causing that light of recognition in your brain you will be reinforcing some pathways in your brain.

Chapter 15: Reduce Large Goals Into

Smaller, More Manageable Projects

Sometimes a person will want to learn a subject, with the best intentions, and a great deal of energy and enthusiasm, only to become disheartened before they even get well and truly started. More often than not, this disheartened feeling is the result of trying to learn a subject that becomes overwhelming in scope. This is particularly true in the case of trying to learn a foreign language. How many people do you know who say time and again how they wish they could speak another language? Or how many people do you know who have started to learn another language but have given up after only a short while? You may actually have experienced this for yourself at one point in time. This is nothing to be ashamed of, rather it is something that is perfectly understandable. The problem with such things as foreign languages is that they are so vast in size and scope that they can seem impossible to learn. Therefore, once the initial excitement of learning a language has worn off a person is left staring this huge monster of a subject in the face, feeling very inferior and incapable of performing the task. That is when most people give up on the thing that they desire to do.

The trick to being able to tackle large learning projects is to break them down to smaller, more manageable pieces. History is full of times where a smaller army was able to defeat a larger, more powerful army. In virtually each and every instance where this happens the simple reason that the smaller army was able to win was that they didn't face the larger army all at once. Instead, they would pick the larger army apart, attacking smaller portions of the enemy time and time again. By splitting the larger army into smaller groups the smaller army is able to outnumber each group that it attacks, giving it the advantage in every encounter. Eventually the larger army is reduced in size and is no longer the threat it once was. At this point the smaller army is now the larger army and it is thus able to finish off the remaining enemy with ease. While you may not be overly interested in military history or strategy this notion of breaking down a large enemy into smaller, more manageable groups is critical for those large learning projects that seem overwhelming. By breaking down the big goal into smaller, more manageable goals you will be able to tackle a large project in a way that doesn't overwhelm you.

One way to achieve this goal, in the case of learning a language, is to simply dedicate a fixed amount of time per day to studying the language. Rather than focusing on the goal of learning the language, focus on the goal of studying the language. As you study you will learn, therefore the important thing is that you apply yourself to the task of studying the language on a regular basis. It is estimated that if a person spends as little as half an hour a day on learning a subject that in one year alone they will have learned enough to be considered an expert in the field. While you may not have the ambition of becoming an expert the fact is that half an hour a day can be all that it takes to tackle a subject as massive as a foreign language. Needless to say, when you think of spending 30 minutes a day on the task then the task suddenly seems far less overwhelming than it might first appear. Therefore, breaking down the overall task into smaller, more manageable goals is the first step toward any great undertaking.

Another way to break down a large task into smaller pieces is to follow a professional guideline. Many foreign language books are broken down into single lessons that are designed to allow you to tackle the whole language in smaller, easier segments. In this way you are only expected to learn so much at any given time. Using the formats provided in workbooks or language courses you can give yourself a framework of smaller, more achievable goals that will eventually add up to accomplish the overall big goal. In the event that such a format doesn't exist for the subject you want to learn you can create it for yourself. Simply break down the material into smaller parts that maintain a natural flow. For example, if you wanted to study baking, then break the subject down into smaller units, such as cakes, pies, savory foods and the like. By focusing on specific categories of baking you can reduce the amount you have to learn at any given time. In the end all of the sections will be covered, and you will have learned all there is to know about baking as a whole.

Chapter 16: Using Guided Meditation To Compliment Learning Techniques

Our brains and bodies are essentially one large camcorder. When we focus our concentration, we are essentially turning on the camcorder. Yet, whether we acknowledge it or not, our internal camcorder is constantly recording the sights and experiences of our world. How does the brain do this?

The brain relies on multiple organs throughout the body to gather the information it uses to create our sense of self and knowledge base. Overtime, the brain can often feel cluttered and make it hard to focus on any new information or skills. Thus, the brain uses various filing systems to essentially purge outdated information and replace it with more up to date facts. Experiences, especially those that received limited attention from us initially, are also often found in the memory's purge file. But for those who want to dig into the memories of their camcorder more intensely, they need a way to enhance their memory to achieve success. New students in the accelerated learning movement are also looking for methods that will help them to achieve a form of clarity, as well as mental enhancement in place of a cluttered camcorder brain and memory.

Meditation is a form of enhancement that can help one to create greater mental clarity. By focusing on moments when learning was successful, one can train the brain to repeat the event over and over again. Meditation assists in recreating these moments. Guided meditation allows for you to walk through specific steps to recreate a mental image of a specific moment in time or a distinct feeling during a period of achievement.

Below are a few of these guided meditations. Please keep in mind that one can create your own or use these. The idea is to tie movements of your body (the physical) with specific feelings and imagery (the mental), which means that you are providing your brain memory aids for digesting new data and other information or skills.

All meditation starts with breathing. It is important to take several slow deep breaths in and out before beginning any meditation. This will help you to relax prior to starting the more intense meditative sessions. While below is one meditation method meant to capture a feeling and associate with a specific physical movement, you can choose other memories and tie them to specific physical movements as well. Thus, this meditation can be adapted to a variety of settings.

Next, remind yourself of a particular experience where your student picked up a particular skill or data set easily. One example could be learning to ride a bike or another physical activity that was easy to pick up. Rebuild that scene of success into a mental image. Put yourself back into that place. Create the scene, include the various background imagery. Fix in your mind how you felt upon the success of that particular experience. Go back there in your mind. Reexperience the success, how it made you feel and how you achieved that success. Provide as much detail as possible, making a complete image and thus really immersing yourself into the experience.

Now capture your feeling of success and pinch your thumb and forefinger together. As the feeling passes, release your fingers. Continue to picture various moments of success. Each time you recreate the feeling of accomplishment, then pinch your thumb together with another of your fingers. Move through the index, middle, ring and finally the pinkie. Finally, pinch all the fingers together with the thumb. Associate this meeting of your fingers and your thumb with the feeling of success. Later, you can pinch your fingers together to remind yourself of that feeling. It can help to create a positive mental environment that is conducive to learning.

Other meditation methods rely on creating a memory aid by attaching a specific feeling or experience to a physical action. Thus, when the physical action is repeated, one can quickly and easily revisit to aid during any learning process. But ultimately, the student's ability to learn anything will be based on the teacher's creating the best possible environment for their students. During any accelerated learning course, an instructor needs to be actively engaging with their students to determine what is successful and what is not.

But how do your students reconnect with you after the accelerated learning course is completed? Followthrough is an important part of any learning course. This gives the instructor a chance to reconnect with their students and find out about their experience with the course. Have they been able to retain what was covered? Has it resulted in a better job performance or has the student been more successful at retaining critical information for specific tests?

The instructor can use follow-up forms to check up on their students. Another method is to add a follow up refresher course for your students. New students can be paired with previous students during the refresher course. This benefits the instructor, because they are able to gauge how well their students retained what they were taught. The students can also build on the social aspects of learning by teaching others, thus cementing it even further into their own brains.

Additionally, reminders geared to reinforce various points of the new skills or data should be used throughout the next few months after the training is completed. The idea is that by using reinforcement, one can keep your students engaged and building upon the original knowledge base they created in your course. However, these refresher options might not always be available. So a course might be geared to include graduates holding mini-training sessions of their own within their specific departments. This saves the company funds, while at the same time, it allows the students to reinforce what they have all been taught.

Accelerated learning relies on many different learning methods, but all of those methods are based on the idea that the student's best learning practices can be found within themselves. Companies in particular can use these accelerated teaching practices to spread new skill sets throughout various departments. How can one do this in a way that is cost effective? Simply put, one needs to keep in mind that training a few students and then allowing them to train others is an easy way to move skill sets through departments without the additional costs of training courses for all the employees.

One example would be to send all the department heads through an accelerated learning course. Then require the department heads to hold mini-sessions within their own departments. It is critical that the department heads employ the teaching methods used in their original course. Thus, these individuals in the position of management will be reinforcing what they have already learned, while saving the company's budget because they are now passing that knowledge on to the next crop of students.

Finally, as we have discussed with meditation, guide your students in various meditation techniques that they can pass on in their own training sessions. Overtime, the company will see the results of memory aids that the students can employ in multiple settings, both within their roles at the company, but also in other areas of their lives were memory retention and gaining new skills is critical.

Chapter 17: Learning To Visualize

I

n this chapter, you will learn why visualizing - i.e., making something visible or depicting something - is so important for our understanding of moderation. Furthermore, we present you some examples of how you can learn, practice and use the technique of visualization.

In this way, even abstract subjects will make it easier to convey them to an audience in an understandable way.

Visualize - what is it?

Two meanings of visualization are important to our understanding:

In general, the visualization of content, in the form of an image or text or a combination thereof.

Specifically, visualization is used to illustrate and clarify something.

The areas of application are very diverse, i.e., you can use the visualization, for example, moderating, presenting or in the knowledge transfer (teaching) excellent.

How do you recognize a good visualization?

Visualizations should direct attention to the essentials. In the figure on the right, the visualization draws our attention to the question to be answered, namely what visualizations mean.

In omission lies the art. Everything unnecessary is to be omitted in visualizations because they should draw attention to the essentials. For this reason, visualizations should not be used to decorate or decorate texts.

Visualizations should be as concrete as possible. The more vivid and lifelike a visualization affects the viewer, the better. He should be able to empathize with the situation that is presented. This applies in particular to graphic visualizations. When visualizing texts, the content should be kept as short as possible. Short sentences - memorabilia memorize our memory better than long and extravagant phrases.

Visualizations should be understandable to others. Here one should avoid using symbols that no one understands and must first be explained. The first illustration visualizes with straightforward means. Everyone who sees the picture will realize it - no further explanations are needed.

Visualizations have to be practiced. A typeface that you can barely read yourself will not invite you to read. Images that are sloppy and unclear are more repulsive than asking. You do not need to be an excellent draftsman to visualize understandable visualizations. You have to know what's important when drawing.

There are many more criteria for good visualization, i.e., the visualization that illustrates. But if you consider the above five criteria in your visualizations, you will get good results. Below is an example of how these five criteria can be visualized as lyrically as possible:

Important points in the eye.

In omission lies the art.

Visualizations should become more concrete.

Visualizations should be comprehensible.

Practice, practice, practice...

These 5 points are easy to grasp at a glance. It is therefore easy to remember them.

Why is visualization so important?

To answer this question, a little digression into our brain is needed. Necessary for our understanding are the following three parts of our brain (evolutionarily seen):

brainstem

Limbic system

cerebrum

We will start with a brief description of the oldest part of the brain and progress to the younger ones. One rule is important in this regard: The oldest parts of the brain must do their work so that the younger parts of the brain can also do their work.

Ie. If disturbances occur in the brainstem, this has an inhibiting effect on the other two parts of the brain.

Brain stem: our survival

The brainstem is the oldest part of the human brain. It is also called the reptilian brain. The brain stem is responsible for breathing, heartbeat, hunger and the sleep-wake cycle, for the instinct - in short, for our survival.

When the brain tells you about disturbances, it affects our understanding. Someone hungry cannot understand or think. If we're lucky, maybe he'll get half of what's happening around him (some research reports about 30% of the ability to absorb). The same applies to fatigue. Those who have not slept enough will not understand much.

Limbic system: feelings and learning

The second oldest part of the brain is the limbic system. It is also called the emotional brain. It is the (control) center for feelings and sexual reactions. Here, the attitudes necessary for all learning and acting have their origin. Without feelings, no action, no learning, no understanding.

It is all the easier to gather information, to learn and to understand, the more it is associated with positive feelings. Pleasant sensations, humor, and personal stories/images therefore have a crucial function. Visualizations can already work here because they make learning easier, and the learning material is associated with positive feelings (possibly with humorous representations).

Cerebrum: saving experience

The evolutionarily youngest part of the brain is the cerebrum. It is much larger in humans than in animals. It accounts for about 85% of the human brain mass. Roughly speaking, its function is to store experiential knowledge and exercise cognitive control over emotional impulses.

The cerebrum is responsible for language, pattern recognition, and creativity. But the prerequisite is always that both the brainstem and the limbic system cooperate, so work.

The areas of the brain where emotions are processed are networked with the parts of the brain needed in logical thinking and vice versa. Reason-oriented thinking is based on brain processes, where not only coherent structures but also emotions play a significant role. It is not the ratio alone that makes man, but spirit and feeling play together.

Visualizations: Images generate feelings

For our understanding, the evolutionary perspective on our brain is important in that we can neither think nor learn nor understand without feelings. Emotions are always linked to pictures. If you remember what you've learned, you're likely to create pictures as well. And you will be able to remember your past feelings, to empathize with them.

Conversely, images generate feelings. Use graphic visualizations to make something clear to yourself or other people.

Of course, that does not just apply to graphic visualizations. Also, stories, metaphors, proverbs, a pictorial language (examples from your own experience), motto, etc. will not only arouse your interest, but also the importance of the other people with whom you are privately and professionally involved. Positive feelings usually accompany arousing interest.

Example: A motto that perfectly fits the topic of this chapter is: "To make you understand, you have to speak to the eye."

Learn to visualize: an observation exercise ...

Read the following little task. It is not difficult to solve. This exercise is primarily about watching yourself find the solution. How exactly do you come up with the solution? Please read only the task. If you have the solution, read on.

Mission: The in-laws of my partner have a son called Erwin. Erwin has brown hair and is an electrician. Erwin has an illegitimate child. What is my relationship to the child?

How exactly did you come up with the solution? Have you imagined people, a specific structure (e.g., a part of a pedigree)? Did you possibly take notes on a piece of paper? For more complex tasks, people like to do so.

They immediately go to the pen to visualize the solution, albeit often in the form of a text. In this case, however, most people are likely to come to the solution without visualizing the text or a structure.

An example of a solution visualization in the form of a text may look like this:

The in-laws of my partner -> these are my parents,

You have a son (called Erwin, Erwin has brown hair and is an electrician -> the description written in parenthesis is unimportant for our job) -> this is my brother.

Erwin has a (illegitimate) child (the one in parentheses is unimportant for our task) -> it is about my nephew or my niece (about the sex is not stated).

Which visualization methods are there?

There are many visualization methods. Here are just a few, commonly used methods that are easy to learn and use...

Family tree - Of course, the structure can also be applied to texts. With the structure of a family, tree hierarchies can be excellently represented - company hierarchies, generic terms, and sub-terms, etc.

Symbols: If you use symbols, make sure they are known. An example of this are the symbols for men or women, which everyone knows.

Clusters: Clusters are great for illustrating ideas that are associatively related. A more detailed description and an example can be found here.

Mindmaps: An example of this. Mindmaps can be used in many ways - in this example, to give yourself and others an overview of the topic.

Lists: Even lists can be applied in many ways from brainstorm to a checklist. You have one example in mind because the visualization methods are placed here in the structure of a list. Make sure, however, that the list is not too long.

Illustrations: Illustrations explain/clarify a text in instructions for use, where the product is pictured, and its components are referred to.

Real objects: they can be relaxing and attuned to the topic. If it is z, for example, a collection of ideas, with the topic - how do we design the garden? - A large basket filled with fruit is a fitting choice. At the end of the meeting, the participants can serve themselves from the fruit basket.

Charts: They work well to illustrate statistics. There are different types of charts: pie charts, bar charts, bar charts, line charts.

Which visualization media are there?

Of course, other tools are important to clarify the content: the visualization media. For one, mostly enough paper. Others prefer their computer to visualize written or pictorial content. Since there are digital cameras, it is no longer a problem to take photos of visualizations, as was done for this chapter.

However, when it comes to imparting knowledge to other people, you should buy appropriate media. The following list is just a short overview:

Blackboard

Tackboard

Flipchart

Whiteboard

Daylight Projector (Overhead Projector)

Slide Projector

Projector

Which medium one chooses depends not only on one's preference but also on which groups of people one has to deal with and which visualization media, for example, in seminar houses, are available. An example: For smaller groups of people (for example up to 10 participants), a flipchart may be sufficient, but for 20-50 people it needs a projector or a medium that can visualize visualizations even from a distance.

Your benefit when visualizing

Visualizations serve to make information easier to grasp. Data is recorded faster and stays in the memory longer. However, depending on the complexity of the topic, repetitions are necessary at regular intervals to get the content into long-term memory. But also repeating content is faster if there are visualizations that illustrate:

Visualizations reduce meetings by up to 30% if the visualizations are well prepared and meet the above criteria.

Visualizations often have a structuring and orienting effect. It's easier to stay on topic. The mind map in Fig. 4 is an example of this.

Visualization seems to clarify, as the view is directed to the essence of the topic. The understanding is easier, but also the notice of knowledge gaps that can be closed by inquiries.

Surely you have several advantages if you have experience with visualizations.

Exercise: How do I get from the text to the picture?

For the following exercise, you only need one pen (pencil is enough) and paper. Read the following exercise. It's about linking a motto with your picture. It's fine if the text appears in the picture itself. But the picture should be more present than the text. The motto is as follows:

"To make you understand, you have to speak to the eye."

Close your eyes and remember the motto. Write down, no matter how crazy, which images/ideas you think of. This should not take more than 5 minutes. Afterward, look at your ideas and select those that seem suitable for visualization. Take a blank paper and record your visualization idea. When drawing yourself, you may come up with good ideas or additions to the original idea. It's good. Experiment - try some visualization ideas until you like them.

It is not easy for many people to come from a text to the picture. However, in this exercise, I was surprised at how many good image ideas people come up with when they embark on the task, even though they had no prior knowledge/experience. However, the exercise was conducted in small groups (2-3 people), which facilitates a collection of ideas.

But as always, practice, practice, practice. The effort is worth it because, with your self-made images to a motto or theme, you will not only arouse your interest but also conquer the hearts of the people.

This is the prerequisite for understanding, namely to create clarity, to make an image - yourself and others.

Chapter 18: How To Improve Memory And Concentration - The Results Will Amaze You!

How frequently have you overlooked very similar things again and again? It appears as though you neglect to accomplish something or lose very identical jobs every week. Wouldn't it be pleasant when you could recollect where you put your eyeglasses or the keys to the vehicle? Shy of placing them in the same spot unfailingly, there ought to be different manners by which you can figure out how to improve memory and focus. This part will talk about a couple of the things that should be possible to enable you to improve your absent-minded ways.

Focus

Fixation and memory are relatively comparative when you consider it. If you recall the majority of the many occasions that you have overlooked where you left your eyeglasses, you may discover that they were not lost since you forgot where you put them, but since you were not focusing on where you left them. A ton of times, individuals make a halfhearted effort of their ordinary assignments without concentrating on what they are doing. If you are acquainted with doing things likewise again and again consistently, for example, perusing and after that taking your eyeglasses off, your psyche mostly dominates and makes a cursory effort for you.

Sooner or later, during this procedure, you are not focusing on what you are doing. Along these lines, losing your glasses cannot be accused of your memory. Consider the rationale. How might you remember something when you were not by any stretch of the imagination focusing around then? One of the main things that you should, when you like to figure out how to improve memory and fixation, is to focus on what you are doing. When this is done, you can proceed onward to different things that will viably utilize the intensity of your mind, yet you must initially figure out how to appropriately deal with it.

Keep Your Brain Fit

Much the same as the remainder of your body, your cerebrum likewise needs to stay fit and sound to work appropriately. This is a significant standard guideline that you should recall whether you wish to figure out how to improve memory and focus. Coming up next are only a couple of the things that you should consider when you are attempting to improve both your mind and fixation:

Exercise Your Mind-Your cerebrum is a muscle that necessities practice to work appropriately. Without a doubt, it is utilized once a day for the more significant part of your everyday undertakings. However, it likewise must be strenuously practiced for it to work taking care of business. For instance, doing straightforward fun and simple assignments, for example, comprehending crossword riddles can assist you with keeping your cerebrum getting it done.

Push your mind to the maximum with regards to your reasoning abilities. The additional push is the thing that you ought to do once a day if you need to figure out how to improve memory and fixation genuinely.

Diminish Stress-Find approaches to lessen your feelings of anxiety. The cerebrum cannot work appropriately when it is exhausted because of your raised feelings of anxiety. In any case, before you can address your issues of not having the option to think and improve your memory, discover what is causing your pressure. Keep in mind that one of the fundamental things that enhance your capacity to figure out how to improve memory and fixation is your capacity to center and focus on what you are doing. If your feelings of anxiety are raised, there is something that is causing a great deal of diversion in your life. Until you deal with circumstances, for example, this, you won't be able to concentrate on different parts of your life, which will consistently forget about you pushed and baffled. Diminishing your feelings of anxiety, and you will find that odds of figuring out how to improve memory and focus will likewise improve.

Unwind Your mind won't perform taking care of business if you are worried and tired constantly. You should discover approaches to unwind. This may be something as straightforward as expanding the measure of time doing fun things that you like to do, for example, investing energy with your family, practicing or shopping. Fundamentally, discovering approaches to build your unwinding time will help in your journey of figuring out how to improve memory and focus.

Diet and Exercise-Contrary to conviction, yet a sound personality and body go close by. Most occasions, when one is undesirable, the other will unquestionably endure also. If you need to figure out how to improve memory and fixation, at that point, you will need to deal with both your body and psyche. Your psyche cannot stay solid if your body is unbalanced. Ensure that you get enough exercise during the day. The cerebrum is just one of the muscles that your body has. You should ensure that different muscles in your body are likewise appropriately worked out.

Notwithstanding exercise, ensure that your body gets the best possible measure of rest and sustenance. The absence of rest will make you feel drowsy, which will, without a doubt, negatively affect your capacity to retain things or concentrate. Eating the off-base sorts of nourishments can likewise make your body respond negatively. Taking specific herbal enhancements, for example, Ginkgo Biloba and rosemary have been connected to improving memory and making you increasingly alert.

Memory Games-Making utilization of memory amusements is an astounding method to enable you to figure out how to improve memory and focus. This can be something as straightforward as utilizing certain traps to recall a person's name. For example, when meeting new individuals, if you imagine that you will experience serious difficulties recollecting that person's name, partner this new person with something that you know about. For instance, does this new person help you to remember something about another person? This would be a brilliant method to review their name later on. Consider something natural that you can connect them with later on.

By and extensive figuring out how to improve memory and fixation ought to be an essential undertaking when you pursue the tips in this part. Keep in mind that before you can recall something, you need to focus on what you are doing. Evacuate the majority of the diversions that ruin your capacity to concentrate on what you ought to do. Figure out how to focus and appropriately deal with your mind. These are the main things that will assist you in learning how to improve your memory and fixation.

Step by step instructions to Improve Memory Recall With Meditation

A lot of items and administrations - drugs or mental medicines - are given to help improve memory review with various impacts. Anybody can see the outcomes with straightforward research of the different medical diaries printed on the web. Pause for a minute to consider this, our progenitors did not have the extravagance or the methods for the created medicines of present occasions, or the medications made today. So if they can improve memory review without anyone else with contemplation systems, for what reason right?

Reflection isn't only exclusively situated in one thing like in prior occasions when they depended on Religious convictions. To pick up capability in thinking, certain practices can be over and overdone. It very well may be difficult for individuals to pick up a fundamental comprehension of how contemplation works, when these individuals cannot appreciate how it capacities, at that point, what more when they need to try it.

Here is a snappy once-over of specific procedures that still show their capacity to be both amazing and viable:

1. Breathing Exercises

This is about the calming rhythm of your body. The clamors a body makes as it takes in and out acts as a basic metronome. The mind at that point unwinds just as conveying more oxygen to the cerebrum and the entire body.

2. Clear Your Mind

A quick-paced world is brimming with duties that cannot be disregarded. There are diversions that we experience, for example, arbitrary contemplations. Commotions or physical requests can likewise go about as outside interruptions.

Just exhausting your brain requires a suspension of faith in outer powers, for example, duties and clamors for at any rate 60 minutes. An hour is sufficient to procure an essential reflective stage.

3. Quiet and Stillness

Individuals basically cannot achieve a meditative state amidst a storm. Commotions and physical requests can be evaded by just heading off to a confined region. Once there, you can do your reflection procedure in harmony.

Improving Memory Retention Through Healthy Habits

Numerous individuals expect that incredible memory is something that usually happens. The facts confirm that a few people may often hold sure musings and can recall data simpler than others. Improving memory maintenance through sound propensities can regularly exceed expectations you to a "skilled" person level in next to zero time by any means.

If you weren't brought into the world with an extraordinary memory, that is okay. I wasn't either. Nowadays, after some training, it's turned out to be much simpler to hold more significant and more prominent measures of data. Possibly you need to have the option to recall straightforward things, for example, where you left your keys, or what bills you have to get paid when. Whatever your explanations behind improving memory maintenance are, these solid propensities will make it much more straightforward.

Exercise

Practice does ponder for your memory. All together for your cerebrum to hold data, it must be in a healthy state. Not to sound prosaism, however being in a solid perspective can mean various things. Ordinary exercise will expand bloodstream and oxygen immersion inside the cerebrum. This will generally prompt improved memory and a general prosperity perspective.

Exercise is incredible for some reasons, and however, concerning the subject of memory, it's imperatively significant. You don't need to work yourself out to weariness, yet a decent 15-20 minutes of cardiovascular exercise will help immensely.

Sufficient Sleep

Keeping up a sound rest example is crucially significant for improving memory maintenance. I wince each time I consider how often I pulled overnighters concentrating for school tests. I can recollect experiencing parts and sections of science and brain research books attempting to pack as much as I could before I went in for the test. I would typically leave an hour or two and no more of rest.

By one way or another, I generally figured out how to do "okay," yet the foggy head I would understanding during the test was unquestionably a piece of information that I would improve a tad of rest.

This applies to regular daily existence too. When you have poor memory, and you feel tired during the day, you could be denying your body and brain of very much required rest. Some of the time 30 minutes to an hour is all you have to get your mind the measure of rest it needs to improve your memory.

Diet

Frequently neglected, your eating regimen can contribute intensely to improving memory maintenance. I won't haul out a long section about how you ought to have one or the other concerning your eating regimen. Anyway, it's imperative to keep your eating routine adjusted.

Have you at any point conversed with somebody that is slimming down in-your-face? A well-known occurrence is reviewed when I endeavored to complete a "low carb" diet. Numerous individuals that deny themselves of specific supplements, protein, starches, or some other piece of a sound and adjusted eating regimen regularly get an overcast personality. Ask anybody that is ever effectively been on a low carb diet for a not too bad measure of time.

This subject can go off digression in all respects effectively so I'll bring it back in and recommend that you keep your eating regimen offset and enhanced with your ordinary nutrient stack.

Following these tips for improving memory maintenance will get you in good shape for recollecting every one of the things you never figured you could! Trust me, and it's much simpler to remember pretty much anything when your body and psyche are sound.

Memory Improvement Supplements

This previous couple of years, sustenance enhancements have been very prevalent as a result of its capacity to improve your general wellbeing and execution, particularly memory improvement. These memory improvement enhancements are delivered utilizing the most normally - happening fixings that have been used by individuals for different purposes for hundreds and thousands of years. When you need to recognize what are these memory improvement supplements that would enable you to help your memory execution, you have unquestionably gone to the perfect spot. I have quite recently the adequate measure of data that would make you go. You don't need to go somewhere else, looking for it on any place you would consider looking through it, sparing you the cerebral pain and the inconvenience that it may cause you only for looking through it yourself. That is without a doubt valid for there are numerous fake sources on the web that may give you poor outcomes instead of the results that are proposed for you by the veritable memory improvement enhancements and items. So why hazard it? We guarantee that when you have wrapped up this article, you would have a clear thought and you would likewise have different choices to browse to improve your memory. So all you need to do presently is no other than: read this cracking article, for the wellbeing of God!

We should get serious. These are the different memory improvement supplements that you could take. Mind you, these are inquired about and demonstrated enhancements, none of these are inadequate so delve in.

Gingko Balboa - this is maybe the most intense enhancement with regards to memory upgrade. It thoroughly causes you to keep up ordinary blood dissemination, particularly on the cerebrum, permitting consistent memory capacities. This is because of the way that blood resembles a vehicle or a taxi inside your veins; it transports stuff, particularly oxygen to your mind so the legitimate course would support you.

Rosemary - no, I'm not discussing your auntie. I'm talking about a similar fixing that you use for flavor in your cooking.

These can be broadly found in the Mediterranean, much more happening than grass. The best thing about rosemary (the herb, not your auntie.) is that it legitimately influences and improves your mind capacities. What I mean about direct is that it doesn't do whatever else like improving blood flow and stuff, it straightforwardly enhances your mind.

Green Tea - this is one of the most widely recognized enhancements and tea drink on the planet at present. It has bunches of advantages, and one of them is, correct, you got it, memory upgrade. It additionally fixes a wide range of illnesses and maladies. Drink this together with dark tea, and you'll get all out wellbeing and memory benefits, ensured.

There are things that you ought to consider before you take this memory improvement enhancement like addicts. Initially, you should confide in specific brands because not all providers can be believed; some are spiked with added substances to cause it to show up bounty so better watch out for that.

What Supplements to Take For Memory Improvement?

In recent years, natural supplements have picked up a great deal of prevalence in improving wellbeing and generally speaking prosperity. Naturally, you can likewise discover supplements gainful for your memory improvement.

Such supplements are created from happening natural substances, and individuals have been utilizing them in various ways for hundreds and possibly a large number of years.

Useful impact of natural supplements on by and broad wellbeing has been all around demonstrated by time and a considerable number of clients.

1) Gingko Biloba Extract is, by all accounts, the supplement that has the best effect on memory improvement. The impact that Ginkgo Biloba has on a body is that it improves the blood course all through your body just as your cerebrum.

Blood is, in addition to other things, an oxygen transportation apparatus for your body, and when your mind has standard, relentless oxygen supply, it works much better.

On the present market, you can discover many various brands offering Ginkgo Biloba Extract. What's more, they all declare that their item is the best. I would recommend you keep with the outstanding, reputable producers.

2) Rosemary is additionally one of the supplements. Rosemary is often utilized as zest, and if you visit the Mediterranean, you can discover it at every progression developing wild.

Mediterranean eating routine is, with the proposal of WHO, THE best eating regimen you can have. As a homegrown supplement, Rosemary's impact is intriguing such that it appears to invigorate the mind capacities legitimately. This is an incredible advantage for memory improvement. Likewise, with Ginkgo Biloba, you can discover several names available so stick with the ones you know and trust.

3) Green tea - typically a large portion of natural supplements gainful for memory

improvement help with your general wellbeing condition too. A good case of this is green tea.

Green tea has in the course of the most recent ten years rose as natural assistance in restoring numerous afflictions and medical issues. Green tea alongside the Black tea is accepted to affect cerebrum capacities helpfully and whenever devoured in moderate portions seems, by all accounts, to be valuable for memory improvement.

4) Ginseng is additionally related to memory improvement. All the time associated with noteworthy energy improvement just as in general body rejuvenation, Ginseng moreover appears to affect memory improved significantly.

Similarly, as with the Ginkgo Biloba and Rosemary keep with the marks you know and trust.

For those of you who have quite recently started to feel memory misfortune signs, likely on account of pressure or age, natural supplements can be the best fix just as aversion for this issue.

Natural memory promoters have fewer reactions than standard memory improvement prescription just as the constructive outcome on your general wellbeing condition.

Step by step instructions to Increase Memory Power - Tips To Boost Your Brain Power

Figuring out how to build memory power can be a baffling procedure for some individuals. Some vibe that individuals, when all is said in done either, have a good memory or don't. Albeit specific individuals do have an inborn capacity to adapt quicker, or hold information, the mind is much the same as a muscle that can be fortified utilizing strategies and activities.

Likely one of the most widely recognized methods for how to expand memory power is by the utilization of mental helpers.

Memory helpers are fundamentally word or picture affiliations which, when contemplated, can help you to remember certain occasions, things, names, and so forth.

Another model is for music understudies who are attempting to figure out how to peruse music. Perhaps you've known about the expression "Every Good Boy Deserves Fudge," or a variety of it. Once more, utilizing the central letters of this mental aide, we can build up the names of the notes on each line of a treble clef — e, G, B, D, and F.

This is the thing that we call a first letter mental aide and can be connected to many circumstances. By working on making your psychiatric aides, you can prepare your cerebrum to search for these quicker, and review them faster.

In the equivalent vain, you can utilize perception methods as methods for how to expand memory control. Once more, this is viewed as a mental aide; however, it makes it so when you think about a specific thing, it will identify with items you wish to recall.

How about we accept learning another dialect, for instance. It tends to be extremely hard to recollect vocabulary, particularly in case you're not in the situation to utilize it every day. Be that as it may, if we use a perception of mental helper, we can prepare our cerebrum to connect pictures with words or expressions.

In Japanese, the expression for "Good Night" is "Oyasuminasai." It sounds such a significant amount of unique about its English partner that it could in all likelihood be hard to recall. In any case, if you somehow managed to consider a picture identified with the expression, for example, a Big full moon on a crisp evening's sky, and afterward think about "oyasuminasai" again and again while as yet envisioning the moon, your mind would perceive that these two relate some way or another. So whenever you attempt to recollect what the Japanese word for "Good Night" is, you would review the enormous moon, and "oyasuminasai."

Notwithstanding mental helpers, you can utilize practices that expansion your fixation, which will likewise incredibly help you on your journey of how to build memory control.

The most straightforward one you can do is known as the "Light Gazing Exercise." With this activity, you permanently light a typical supper flame and spot it about a manageable distance far from your body in an obscured room. You need it to be at around eye level.

Presently, close your eyes and clear your brain as well as can be expected. When you are prepared, open your eyes and look at the flame without squinting. Attempt and spotlight on the light, however much as could reasonably be expected. When your eyes to begin to water and you want to look, close your eyes and attempt and picture the flame.

In this state, you should attempt to recollect all the little subtleties of the flame. From the outset this will be troublesome as you aren't prepared at this point, so don't be debilitated if the light appears somewhat fluffy in your psyche.

After a couple of minutes, open your eyes again and look at the light. Rehash this procedure for in any event 20 minutes every day. The more you practice, the better your focus, which is a crucial segment when attempting to figure out how to build memory control.

Five Suggestions on How to Increase Memory Power

We need our memory to work in our day by day lives. Without it, we can't recollect realities, what we are doing straightaway or significant occasions that occurred in our lives. Since memory is so substantial for day by day life, what would one be able to do if they are experiencing difficulty with it? The five thoughts beneath can help tell the best way to build memory control.

1. Keep away from Certain Foods

There are a few nourishments that are extraordinary for improving memory. Fish is one of these sustenances. Others incorporate the natural product, high-cocoa content chocolate, vegetables, dairy, and oats. This is because they are low on the glycemic list (GI). Sustenances low on the GI takes more time for your body to separate, so they help keep your memory continually dynamic.

A few kinds of sustenances and beverages do the inverse for memory. These sustenances are on the opposite finish of the GI. While OK with some restraint, liquor, soft drink, white bread, and sugars can diminish memory, so lessening the measure of these sustenances in a single eating routine can build memory.

2. Remain Physically Active

Since you increment your body's bloodstream when you work out, you likewise increment bloodstream in your mind. This can support memory. When you ceaselessly remain dynamic, your cerebrum will as well.

3. Exercise your Mind

Riddles, similar to crosswords and computer game secrets, can improve memory. By "practicing the brain," you can strengthen its exhibition for different errands. Developing aptitudes with riddles proposes improvement in memory and cerebrum work.

4. Use Supplements

Omega 3-unsaturated fats can support memory. They explicitly improve cerebrum capacity, center, and correspondence between synapses. Fish contains these acids, as do fish oil and flaxseed oil supplements. Different supplements for memory are Ginkgo Biloba, folic corrosive, and sage oil.

5. Get Rest

If you get to rest, your memory will work better. Rest and unwinding help your mind work appropriately. Sleeping, contemplation, and breathing activities likewise improve memory.

Chapter 19: Setting Your Goals

To get the maximum results from this book, it would be helpful to not only look at each chapter as its own tip for self-discipline; you should also take in the entire thing as one cohesive entity. Given this, I think that a brief recap of what we've covered so far in chapters 1 - 4 is in order.

In chapter 1, we discussed what self-discipline is, where it comes from, and why, to become a more focused person in this life, it matters as a skill. In chapter 2, we looked at how building your own personalized schedule and sticking to it are of the utmost importance when it comes to maintaining your self-discipline so you don't just flail willy-nilly towards whatever it is you want. Next, in chapter 3, we focused on how avoiding excess and keeping balance in your self-disciplined life will help you to continue walking the straight and narrow path without falling back into your old ways. Finally, in chapter

4, we discussed the huge difference between motivation and discipline, and how being able to recognize the difference will ensure that your productivity is not short-lived.

With all of the information thus far, you should have a solid base with which to start practicing self-discipline. I would also say that this final chapter could be seen as optional, but I hope you're willing to power through to the end (as a newly self-disciplined person, you should have no qualms about this) because it is my hope that this last section will give you some key insight into how you can channel your knowledge from chapters 1-4 into your own personal goals.

Throughout this book, I've made frequent references to the varying hopes, dreams, and aspirations of every man, woman, and child on this planet. This chapter will be no exception. Here we will focus on building self-awareness so you can look inside yourself to discover what your own individual goals are and how you can begin the process of achieving them with the greatest success.

While childhood days may have provided us with many ideas of the things we would like to accomplish in life, (becoming an astronaut, doctor, cowboy, to name a few select careers) the stages of late adolescence and adulthood tend to give the majority of people a drastically changed perspective. This, of course, isn't anyone's fault. The world just operates differently than most people think when they lack any informative worldly experience. As a child, many of us are used to having things given to us, so when adulthood hits, we are shocked to find that not only does society not really care about what we want, it seems to actively be trying to keep us from that desire.

Again, this isn't any one person's fault, but rather it's everyone's. Almost every single person is trying to accomplish something, or get something, and so it stands to reason that at some point, two people with a common goal will try to get the same thing when there's really only enough for one of them – be it a job, or a romantic partner, or anything really. What the result of this tends to be, more often than not, is that the person with the least amount of dedication and self-discipline will fail while the other will attain the success that both originally pined for.

This isn't to suggest that a person – any person – couldn't accomplish these aforementioned goals if they really wanted to (although, a cowboy might not be exactly what the person was expecting since there's a lot more herding involved), it's just that usually, they are faced with the problem we discussed in the previous chapter: motivation. They have a starry-eyed view of the potential job or girl they've been crushing on, but they only see the end result. As if they time traveled, they picture themselves in the glorious career or with that beautiful woman, and they envision themselves accomplishing these things without really taking into account all of the dedication and focus that is a pre-requisite to get there in the first place.

Again, that initial spark could be seen as necessary, because without those starry-eyed young adults who dared to dream, our society would certainly collapse. We would find ourselves with a dangerous deficit of doctors, lawyers, and cowboys. But again, the only people who end up making it in those roles are the ones with self-discipline, because again, it isn't just about having the desire to do something; it's having the dedication to back that desire.

With this in mind, I want you to take one minute to think about one of your own individual goals. Whether it was one you had when you were younger or one you currently have, just take sixty seconds to consider it. Think specifically why you might've failed up until now to accomplish it. I'll wait.

Did you do it? Because I did. And what I found is likely what you found too: that the goal's end result was something you desired, but the path to arrive there wasn't fleshed out enough for you to begin taking the steps to begin traveling down it.

From here on out, I'll outline three sequential tips to help you move past this mistake so that you can actually start to have an idea of what it is you need to do.

1. Narrow that goal down

A big problem that many people face when trying to reach a certain goal is that the goal itself is way too broad. Someone says, "I want to be a doctor" or "I want to play the guitar" but he doesn't take into consideration that these are just umbrella terms. Does he want to be a surgeon? A pediatrician? An anesthesiologist? Does he want to learn the electric guitar? Classical guitar? Does he want to be able to play solos or just chords?

These are all questions one needs to ask themselves before embarking towards any goal. If you don't, you'll likely find yourself at a crossroads of options without a good idea of which direction you want to take.

2. Break it up

Alright, so after you've narrowed down what you want to do, you need to devise your plan of attack. This, to reiterate, is what will set you apart as a self-disciplined person: you have your desire and your plan to make it a reality. It might feel good to have finally decided what it is you want to do, but don't pat yourself on the back too much. And, more importantly, don't even try and see the ultimate finish line, because this is a very good way to get discouraged fast by the amount of work that's ahead of you.

A good amount of people might disagree with me here, as they think that an "eyes on the prize" approach is best. You can see in your mind's eye what it is you're working towards and, as a self-disciplined person, this is okay, because you'll get there eventually right? Well, not quite. If you take away anything from this book, I would hope you'll see the fallacy in such thinking. Yes, you need to have an idea of what the end result of all your hard work will be (otherwise, how would you know what you're trying to do?) but it is absolutely imperative that you avoid such long-term thinking and try to divide the ultimate goal up into smaller goals so you don't get burned out. Going back to chapter 4, you need to see the accomplishment of your goal as a marathon that will take a lot of time and pacing – not a sprint you can just arrive at after pushing yourself for a brief period.

6:1 rule

When you decide on a goal – whatever it is – and once you narrow it down, it is helpful to consider it is as not one big goal, but a clumped collection of smaller goals. These individual checkpoints will allow you take things slower to ensure that you're making the best possible progress that you can.

Depending on what your goal is, it could have twenty, or even hundreds of smaller goals within it. But for the sake of time, I think the 6:1 rule tends to work sufficiently enough. Let's go back to the example of learning to play the guitar. Your 6:1 might look something like on the next page:

1:          The   Overall   Goal:
I want to learn to play the electric guitar

The 6 individual steps to making that happen
You obtain the guitar and amp.
You decide if you want to take lessons from a teacher, or maybe just learn from tutorials online.
You write out your practice schedule.
You stick to the schedule.
You learn your first song.
Revise.
Of course, once you finish your first run-through of the 6:1, the final step is that you need to actively revise it. For the guitar example, say, once you learn that first song, you need to decide if your practice schedule is still working for you. Or, if you're paying a teacher for lessons, maybe you've reached the point where you can start learning better on your own. That's the best part of having smaller goals to break up the larger one – you're not beholden to any one way of doing things,

and you can try different things to find the best possible option for you as an

This brings us to our final point of this chapter: the beauty of change. Society and the people within it are in almost constant flux. You could almost argue that life itself is really only about change, so why are people so adamant about staying the same? By making the choice to be more self-disciplined, you are literally making an effort to change, so why, with our goals, do we oftentimes refuse to budge on them? This is something that tends to happen in young adults as they grow into adulthood. They have their specific goals, but they don't allow those goals to change as they do, and what ends up happening is they become discouraged by their failure to achieve any sort of success and give up pursuing other long-term goals in the future.

I'm definitely not saying that you should change your goals entirely if they are something you're set on because, with self-discipline and hard work, anything is possible. But what I am saying is that to avoid become discouraged, you need to maintain not only a dedicated outlook towards your goals but also a realistic outlook that informs you if the given goal can actually be attained in the first place.

For example, if you want to be a famous actor but you don't want to move away from your hometown to New York or Hollywood, you will wind up with few options to go about reaching that goal.

It's important to remember that it's okay to have multiple, overarching goals that you're slowly attacking at once; it's good not to carry all your eggs in one basket, so they say. Sure, you can have one goal whose attainment you want the most, and it can be one where the majority of your free time is going; but it's also wise to not get boxed into one thing. It's okay to spend half an hour less on your main goal and dedicate it to one of your alternates. What I've found is that spending even this small of an amount of time can give you some previously unseen insight into your alternate goal, and you might find that you enjoy this other goal so much that it becomes your main one!

The big thing to take away here is that not only does everyone have different goals, but that over time, your own goals are likely to change. It's also important to remember that this is okay, and as long as you continue to build your good self-disciplined habits, you can take on any disappointment of a particular goal that doesn't pan out, because you have the training and drive to move on to the next thing that just might wind up a success.

Chapter 20: The 'Why' Of Nlp

In a world where multitasking and spreading oneself thin over a plethora of activities have become all the rage, a program like NLP, scientifically devised and tested for optimum results, takes a front seat when it comes to self-development and improvement of one's own brain and its capacities. In this chapter, we will explore how the techniques involved in the NLP program can be best utilized and exploited in order to reap maximum benefits out of it.

Like most ideologies implemented in life, NLP practitioners believe that it is not WHAT you do that brings you success, but HOW you do it. Irrespective of the nature of the job being done, if done with 100% efficiency guarantees optimum results. Structure takes priority over content, and heavy focus is laid on getting the job done with minimum effort, maximum efficiency and optimum time.

NLP teaches us to quit worrying about making money, and instead divert all the energy spent into that towards more fruitful activities such as long term planning, analyzing how money can be efficiently invested, recognizing and opening themselves to opportunities and honing the skills needed to identify great investments.

The common man will perceive money as being the sole trouble in his life, and will thereby treat himself as a victim to the trap of money. However, with the help of NLP, we can re-model our thinking so that we are no longer the victim in this rat race, and change a certain view we might hold in our mind about ourselves. When we imagine ourselves to be helpless, we are effectively ensuring in generating a mindset which will further promote and cultivate deep rooted feelings of helplessness, in turn fulfilling the unconscious's prediction of becoming helpless. This is what is known as a "vicious cycle".

However, when we apply the concepts of NLP and channelize our mind to think in a particular direction about us, we learn how to control our thought process. We are also able to clearly perceive and recognize obvious money making schemes, giving us the courage needed to take the risk and hence reach out for chances which money may provide. As NLP has designed the mid to turn any digging field into a mine of opportunities, three states of the mind therefore engage in ensuring that any decision taken with regards to money is implemented with the highest level of accuracy and precision, hence ensuring excellent results.

Seasoned veterans in the practice of employing the techniques of NLP to money making confide that all that is required is a change from the negative mindset associated with money, to a more positive one, where new ideas are embraced and welcomed. Negative beliefs and thoughts about money need to be avoided in order for the NLP to work. Apart from this, it isn't just about seeing yourself in a rich position. It also helps to find out how people in influential and higher positions handle their money, as well as the attitude they adopt when dealing with money. Money should be regarded as the natural counterpart of building business relationships and offering services to wealthy people.

Once the human mind has been trained to perceive money as a stepping stone for success, and not as a weak link to failure, it can be conditioned to analyze the different methods and measures which can be taken to amplify the money which one has in one's hands into larger, enormous amounts. NLP also incorporates a sense of being better able to handle earned money. As is often the case, many times people who earn huge amounts blow it all away, by not being resourceful and practicing sustained spending. This is a downward spiral, which sucks out all enthusiasm and effort needed to maintain a streak of positivity with respect to money making. NLP conditions the mind to implement wise, well thought out expenditure plans, and carrying out savings plans also becomes a much easier task when coupled with the norms laid down by the NLP program.

Once all this has been achieved, money management comes into the picture. The instinct which tells you whether to invest in a particular project, or whether running a risk of losing some money to make a profit out of it later on is worthwhile, such instincts can be honed and perfected with the help of the NLP techniques. As explained before, NLP trains the mind to dwell deep into the unconscious to help in improving the accuracy of these instincts and better the predictability of a situation.

As you can see now, there are various methods and tricks which can be implemented, all part of the NLP program, which will forever change the way you look at and think about money. Once this happens, the sky is the limit. However, there are a few precautions needed to be taken to ensure that desired results are achieved. We will be exploring these cautionary measures in the next chapter.

Chapter 21: The 'Don'ts' Of Nlp

Since there are no harmful effects to the NLP, it is expected that some side effects will present themselves over the course of the method. However, this is not the case. But a few precautionary measures need to be taken nevertheless when dabbling with NLP, which prevent the plan from going awry resulting in disastrous end outputs.

As the foundation for the program rests on the concept of comparison, it is important to not go overboard by over estimating other people or undermining one's own capacities, as this leads to a complete derailment of the purpose of the program. Holding oneself on a high pedestal can also have derogative effects, as self-criticism is an important feedback review measure for any self-development scheme.

NLP primarily focuses on the control of emotions, and feelings through controlling measures. NLP helps in achieving focus and organization, by controlling emotions and actions. However, this must done within limits, as a complete lack of emotions will make a person cold and insensitive and spoil one's relations and connections with people. Overusing them or displaying them in inappropriate situations hinders progress, and thus needs to be avoided. Be the boss of your mind, don't let it boss you.

Focus is key to getting results out of the program, so it is imperative to have a clear goal in mind before beginning. Goals may be altered, as mentioned before, however too many alterations can lead to a confused and befuddled mind. Once a goal has been set, try to focus on achieving the goal in its original form, rather than modifying it according to your whims. NLP is a scientific program, functioning on analysis of facts, and as such should be approached as one.

Do NOT expect results on the very first day of the program. The NLP program works according to one's capabilities and the time taken for results to be exhibited varies from person to person, as each human is wired differently. Hence, raising your expectations might lead to disappointments and a diminishing enthusiasm, which could prove disastrous for mind control. Shortcut methods and distractions need to be avoided at all costs, as this will only further hinder the progress of the program

Conclusion

I would like to thank you once again for getting this book and reading up to this point. The fact that you have read until the end of this book tells me that you are really serious in learning about the art and skill of speed reading. That is a good thing. And I assure you that if you apply every piece of advice and technique contained in this book, there is absolutely no reason why you won't increase and improve your reading and comprehension skills. Most of the tips and techniques discussed here are very practical. Anyone can do them. It may take some time for you to get used to them but you will, sooner or later. It's just a matter of practicing the techniques whenever you have the time.

It's my goal that this book will help you achieve the reading and comprehension skills that you've always aimed for. If you think you have missed something, I recommend that you get back to the book and re-read the section or sections that you didn't understand that well. Sometimes, it's necessary to read a chapter twice or even thrice to fully understand its meanings and lessons. I suggest that you keep a copy of this book accessible so that you can easily review it whenever you want. This book is easy to copy and store. You can have it saved in your mobile phone for hassle-free access. .

www.ingramcontent.com/pod-product-compliance
Lightning Source LLC
Chambersburg PA
CBHW060333030426
42336CB00011B/1324